*To all those people who at one time or another
have wanted to try a new craft,
but have never thought they could possibly succeed.*

CONTENTS

PREFACE
From Temptation to Reality

I would love to! But how could I possibly do that? Are you crazy?

Sometimes it's an exhibition. Sometimes it's a friend. Or a picture in a magazine or an appealing piece of art in a shop-front window. From what you see comes an inspiration and a nice warm fuzzy feeling. And then the temptation, "Wouldn't it be great to do something like that?" Following which the inspiration so predictably disappears amid a sigh of self-imposed resignation. After all, you couldn't possibly contemplate even *trying* to have a go at something like woodcarving or wood sculpture. Of course not.

You are hopeless with your hands? Of course you are. You can't draw? Of course you can't. And you don't know which end of a chisel to hold? Silly you. Sharpen it? Are you kidding? You mean you didn't do any good at art in school? Had to do math instead? But you knew someone who did and she really made some great stuff?

None of those? Then the real reason is you haven't got a workshop? No time either? And it is all too expensive?

Hey, how could you possibly do woodcarving anyway if you can't cut a straight line with a saw or hammer in a nail without belting your finger?

Funny, isn't it? Here you are one minute thinking how you would like to give something like woodcarving a go and all you can come up with is 101 reasons why you shouldn't even try!

If this describes you, *then this book is for you.*

THIS BOOK WILL CHANGE YOUR MIND

This book will turn your seeming pipe dream and your assumed "can't do" into the envy of all your friends. This book will take you from your very first cut with a knife right through all the learning processes needed to display your new artistry. If you follow the path this book maps out for you, you will never look back, except with the smile of achievement. You will move further and further away from a past of self-doubt and closer to a future of fulfillment and pride.

It is of great importance that we take some time out now, right at the very beginning, to see just what it is that makes us think we can't even "have a go" at woodcarving. Each of us will have reasons that will vary considerably; however, all of the reasons will be equally valid to each of us individually.

If your specific reason or reasons are not actually covered here, chances are there are one or more that come very close. With a little reading between the lines, and some careful lateral thinking, it is most likely that you will be able to work through your reasons and justify why you really *should* give woodcarving a go.

To help us determine some of these reasons for our assumed inability to even think we are capable of successful woodcarving, we need to step back in time and go over some of the conditioning processes we have gone through . . .

Children in their beginning years are mostly the same the world over. Energetic. Bubbly. Boisterous. Fearless. Inquiring. They absorb new knowledge even faster than they can eat. They want to know and need to know. Everything.

Playschool, preschool, primary school, high school, college, and university. TV. Computers. Outer space and inner space. The lot is consumed by children and young adults with an insatiable devouring of things that are new.

The gathering of knowledge is, for today's person, an extraordinary process of bombardment of all things imaginable. A never-ending and forever broadening array of bits and pieces of information—opinions, educated guesses, facts, and fiction.

And all along throughout this barrage, today's person, just like yesterday's person and tomorrow's person, is being cajoled, and pushed, and prodded, and guided, and coerced, and sometimes straight out shoved toward, and down, the path of their life. Sometimes it is the life path they want, sometimes they might prefer a different one, and very often it just happens. It evolves from circumstance and things at points in time that are simply to be or not to be. Some might call this fate, and others may never consider a name for it at all.

Whatever all these things are that make the stuff of life, whether planned or unplanned, there is one outcome that is inevitable. And that is that, no matter what a person's natural instincts and inclinations are or when he or she was born, all these impinging bits and pieces of information will change the person over time. They will make that person what he or she is, and will influence what he or she does as time forever marches on.

When we are tempted as children, little do we think about the consequences of what we do. We very often do things without a thought about their importance or how they might change our lives or how they might change someone else's life. We do things because we "want to." Or because of peer pressure. Or because we were asked to do it, or maybe even told to do it. For the most part we trust those around us not to react unfavorably, so we just do things within the confines of our limited reasoning, without fear or knowledge, and with limited personal understanding.

As children we explore, we create, we fantasize, and we imagine the most impossible things; and we wonder in quizzical fascination at just about everything around us. Notice the words explore/create/fantasize/imagine/wonder/quizzical fascination. If someone says, "Here's how you dig a hole in the sand," we have a go, too. Or maybe it's drawing a tree. Or sanding some wood. Or doing some carving.

In my studio, I teach children from age six years to carve wood. They do both relief carving and carving in the round. I have never yet had a child who had done anything like it before he or she started woodcarving in one of my classes, so none of them had ever had prior experience in this craft. I have never had one child even hint in the slightest way that they "could never do that," and I have never had one child fail to achieve, with pride, a present for Mom or Dad.

Now in itself that isn't particularly remarkable. What is remarkable is that if I have a teenager come to my studio with an examination project that needs some carving on it, the teenager is unable to project the same enthusiastic inquiring mind and quizzical fascination as the six year old. There is already too much "logic" that

inhibits the process of creation by manual skill. There is already too much time pressure. Too much negative peer influence. Too much rush to finish and not enough appreciation that fine results in art are achieved by sustained and deliberate acts during which our personal creativity flows freely.

So it is with even less surprise that by the time our twenties are reached self-doubt is well formed. The late twenties and into the thirties are, for some, child raising and homemaking years. Interest in many skill-related activities is minimal because they are often impossible—and, needless to suggest, this also presents the perfect excuse to avoid succumbing to temptation and to hide behind yet another reason why we mustn't try.

For the vast majority of us, for most of our formative years, we are subjected to a compulsory education system, which has a great and probably permanent influence on our future lives. As we move out of this compulsory education system, many of us use the information it has provided us to make decisions about further education. And so already the influence of our early years is significantly molding the long-term path of our lives.

Education systems inevitably channel thinking, and therefore have a great responsibility for the way in which we organize and deal with our lives. On top of this, life itself is taking up ever increasing amounts of our time. Work, housing, and family are just some of the major consumers of our time and energy. We begin to get so caught up in these life issues that for many of us there is often little other focus.

Unless a part of our life includes a focus on our personal development as part-time or hobby artist, it is no surprise that we form a low opinion about our ability to become competent artists.

The longer this lasts, it seems the more remote become our personal beliefs in the potential for ourselves to be able to follow an artistic pastime such as woodcarving or wood sculpture. We could say then that unless our education includes an artistic strand, and unless for whatever reason we undertake or at least try an artistic activity sometime after our formal education is completed, we are less likely than ever to turn artistic temptation into reality. If we were not naturally artistically inclined as children, then our educational and social conditioning not to be so is even more effective.

THE TWO FEAR BARRIERS

Irrespective of whether we have simply been tempted to have a go, or we have actually just started to experiment in woodcarving or wood sculpture, if we have never done it before, there is one common characteristic in us all. It is fear. I am not a psychologist, but I have seen barriers potential carving students have that can be attributed to fear of one kind or another.

The "fear barrier" is very real, and it is very effective for thwarting the personal development of artistic skill. It is also very much a removable barrier which, given the right set of circumstances, will never return.

The "fear barrier" that has developed within ourselves for woodcarving represents the end result of the relevant things that have impinged upon us during our formal and informal education. In my experience as a teacher, these fear barriers are never there in children with regard to woodcarving! There are two categories of fear barrier about woodcarving, both of which have the same end result. The first fear barrier is the one that prevents us from believing that we should even try our hand at the craft, the end result being not to attempt it at all. The second fear barrier emerges after we have begun, causing us to flounder and give up before the fear is overcome.

Let's take them each in turn:

First—The "I Could Never Do That" Fear Barrier

If you are attracted to the concept of woodcarving but dismiss it as an impossible or ridiculous dream, you fit the "I could never do that" category of fear.

You reject accepting the opportunity to try because you believe, consciously or subconsciously, that you are incompetent with your hands (most likely because a teacher at school said so), and/or you have no artistic ability, and/or you have no knowledge of anything to do with it. These notions may be coupled with a fear of making a fool of yourself in front of other people. You might believe other people may think it so out of character for you to be woodcarving that "you must be joking." So that you don't appear to others to be associated with any of these situations, you may be inclined to use as your reasons for not "having a go" things like "I don't have the time" or "I don't have the space."

In our opening paragraph to this section, the words "If you are attracted to the concept of woodcarving" were used. It is this original emotion that is the critical signal that indicates both your want and your need to have a go at woodcarving. The presence and recognition of this signal should now become your greatest encouragement to step over your fear barrier. This is for two fundamental reasons—first, your attraction to it has uncovered a latent desire; and, second, there is nothing in the act of woodcarving that you are incapable of doing because it is a relatively uncomplicated activity, albeit there are many facets to it.

Your fear is, in truth, based on ignorance which can be removed by learning, plus past conditioning by others as to particular manual or artistic incompetence, with the inference that such a thing should not be tried, when in fact it is a relatively simple task. If you believe you are up against this fear barrier, then *this book is for you.*

Second—The "I'm Trying to but I Can't Do This" Fear Barrier

If you are already trying your hand at woodcarving or wood sculpture, and there is nervousness or anxiety associated with one or more of the following, you have "I'm trying to but I can't do this" fear.

You don't know what to do next or you are afraid of breaking something off or "mucking up" what you are trying to do or what you are doing doesn't "look right."

Associated with this fear barrier is the common pattern that if nothing changes soon, you will most likely give up your new art. Your experience of this fear may also stay with you for some time, making it unlikely you will try this or another art form in the near future. You might feel incompetent, disillusioned, confused, or generally lacking a direction, and feel like you are wandering aimlessly around your piece of wood. The reaction of *"I'm trying to but I can't do this"* is a natural and perfectly normal response to your feelings as you experience this fear barrier.

This fear is, in truth, also based on ignorance, which can be removed by learning the right steps for a relatively simple task. In some ways you are more fortunate than the person facing the *"I could never do that"* fear barrier, because you have already crossed the line and started the activity. It is just that if you don't get help soon, you will be less fortunate because you will have tried and failed, and this is ultimately worse than not trying at all. At least in not trying, the fantasy of doing woodcarving or wood sculpture remains potentially alive. If you try and fail, not only does the fantasy die, so does the likelihood of your further interest in another art form.

So if you believe you face this fear barrier, *this book is for you too.*

WHAT SOME PEOPLE THINK & SAY ARE MYTHS THAT UNKNOWINGLY CREATE FEAR

As with many activities, for successful woodcarving to happen there are things that are necessary, whether they are already there or need to be learned, and myths that need to be dispelled. Here are five myths that should not be allowed to stand in your way:

Myth 1—You Need to Be Artistic

If ever there was a myth about doing woodcarving it is this one. Being artistic may well be a natural part of some people's makeup, but it is not a prerequisite to being able to do some "nice stuff." Having some artistic appreciation is more the requirement, and this can be learned as we discuss later.

In fact, when you couple some artistic appreciation with some simple carving, you will all of a sudden be perceived as artistic! There often seems to be a perception that for art, one needs to be an artist before one can do it. It is rather silly in reality, as one cannot generally be an artist without learning the craft first!

When the words "I can't" are used, they often really mean "I haven't learned to do that." Unfortunately we don't express it that way; so we interpret it as a "cannot do" activity.

As you follow through this book, you will learn the necessary art to be able to be "artistic." Of the fundamental arts, some drawing skill needs to be learned as well as some visualization skill.

Myth 2—You Need to Be Really Good with Your Hands

It is true that to produce intricate works of woodcarving one needs to have well-developed motor skills. Manual dexterity, like artistic ability, is more naturally present in some people's makeup than in other's. However, motor skills are also learned skills, so the person with a low natural ability can also become one with a well-developed ability.

The learning of manual skill can be a fun experience, to the extent that one isn't really aware that one is "learning" at all, or it can be hard labor with doubtful results. The latter is generally a result of the wrong projects at the wrong time with the wrong guidance, and just to top it off, the inadequate teacher in whom you have placed your trust tells you your vocational prowess must not include doing anything with your hands. Those of us who were "hopeless with our hands" at school were most likely victims of the "teacher's copout." *If this is you, this book is definitely for you.*

Myth 3—You Need to Be Strong to Do Woodcarving

You *do* need to have good natural hand strength to do large sculpture; however, you do not need to be strong to create fabulously detailed relief carving and smaller sculptures.

The choices of the pattern, the tools (especially the mallet), and the wood are the deciding factors for the required hand strength. Someone with arthritis in the hands can do woodcarving if the choices are correct. Of course it may depend on the degree of arthritis, and one's medical advice.

In times gone by, in many English-speaking countries, relief woodcarving was the preferred pastime for housebound women with time on their hands. Some extraordinary carvings were achieved. Woodcarving certainly was not the preserve of "strong men" except in the area of the journeyman tradesperson. There are greater choices of timber species and better tools and equipment than were ever available in the past; these all allow for more flexibility and greater opportunity.

Myth 4—You Need a Lot of Tools

A professional woodcarver may have two or three hundred woodcarving tools in the workshop. For most of the time, this professional will use maybe a couple of dozen. For the kind of work a hobbyist will do, these same couple of dozen are more than adequate.

Start with two or three tools only, and build as you go. Tool-buying can be addictive and a lot of fun, but modern tools can be expensive; so it is important to purchase only those you really need, and this means buying tools individually rather than in sets, which may include tools you will never use. The carving in Chapter 1 is created with just a simple knife. Buying on a needs basis first, getting to know what they are all about, and enjoying each new purchase as it comes.

Each tool has an amazing versatility of its very own; so exploit this characteristic, and you will soon see just how few you really need.

Myth 5—You Need to Know All about Wood

The greater the knowledge about wood the better off you *might* be, not *will* be. The key factors are *where* to go to get the greatest choices of wood and, when you come across a piece of wood, *what* characteristics you need to look for to help decide its suitability for a particular design. You do not need to know its common name, its botanical name, where it comes from, what it is used for commercially, or anything else about it. You only need to know what to look for in it.

As the chapters progress, we will examine more and more about wood and its characteristics. We should always bear in mind that wood is a naturally formed organic mass of cells that conforms to certain characteristics within a species. Every piece can be different, depending on many factors. Its behavior under a chisel can vary from one side of the tree to the other, and one end of the tree to the other.

A woodcarver needs to get to know wood from the point of view of working with it. This can only come with experience, and that can only come from exposure to it over time. Knowing all about wood is not a prerequisite to starting carving. Learning about wood happens as a natural outcome of the process of doing carving.

SOME THINGS IT IS HELPFUL TO HAVE

The learning of a manual skill and the application of it to an art form is not something that naturally occurs overnight. Some people may adapt to things more quickly than others, and some people may find certain aspects of the craft more difficult than others.

Patience

It is important to give yourself a chance to give it a try. Younger people tend to be naturally more in a rush to get things done; this is often to the detriment of the long-term success of their art.

Art needs thinking time. It needs planning time, and it needs time for its subtleties to be exploited by the artist. In most instances these subtleties are not evident at the beginning of the "doing" process. They become apparent as the work progresses, and it is during this process that the experience of the artist bears fruit.

No one should have an expectation that from day one their carving will be fast to do and look stunning. However, if one takes the process step by step, and chapter by chapter, there will be a fulfilled expectation that carving will become easier and easier, and look better and better in a reasonable time.

An Inquiring Mind

If you have an inquiring mind when it comes to things about art, wood, and tools, then you are well on the way to being a successful practitioner of woodcarving.

The more inquisitive you are, the easier your learning process will be, and the more satisfying the results from the time you put in. Some of the great attributes of creating art from wood come from three things:

Because it is an art form, the only limitation to design is one's *imagination*;

Because wood is a natural organic substance, its *characteristics* are limitlessly variable;

Because the nature of hand tools is "addictive ownership," there is an endless amount of *enjoyment* working out which one to get next!

Each of these characteristics offers an insatiable supply to any inquiring mind.

A Small Space with a Stable Work Surface

Unless you are working in large sculptures or relief carvings, there is no requirement for a large workspace. A small number of tools can be stored in a tool roll or box, and the wood you are working on will determine the workspace size. The only essential is that the work surface is stable and does not wobble. The table or bench will need to be reasonably solid so that it doesn't move if a mallet is used with the chisel. The table need not be heavy, but it does need to be well made.

Woodcarving is an activity that is highly portable. Do it inside or outside, or take it on holidays with you. Make or buy a folding table; then you are completely self-contained and mobile.

POSITIVE THINGS YOU WILL DEVELOP THROUGH CARVING

As your carving experience grows, there are some accrued benefits that are transferable to all sorts of other activities. Some of these are:

Development of Objectives
Many a time, we want to do something, but we don't quite know what. We are not quite sure what it is that really interests us, how we want something to look, or even why we want to do it! Mostly this is because we have not developed our objectives clearly enough.

Sometimes the development of objectives can't be done effectively because we aren't aware of what the alternatives are, and how to go about exploiting them. This book will expose you to a considerable variety of alternatives, each of which can be combined in many different ways to make unlimited carving possibilities.

This book will also encourage you to focus on different aspects of each carving, and this will in turn enhance your ability to determine what it is you really want to do with it.

Development of Your Observation Ability
One of the most common discoveries we make when we start out to carve is that what we thought we knew we don't really know at all.

You know what a horse looks like? Of course you do! But can you draw one? No? Why not? Because in truth you don't know the detail, the proportions, the placement of its body parts, of a horse! If you have normal motor skills, then the only thing stopping you from drawing a horse is knowledge about what it actually looks like. This kind of knowledge comes from observation. Try copying a picture of a horse (without tracing it), and you will soon discover how far we need to go to develop our observational skills.

This book will show you how to take those skills to another level; very soon you will be looking at things in an amazingly different way to how you have been all your life.

Development of Creative Thought Process
Expressions such as "I am not artistic" or "I am not creative" will become negative statements of the past.

As you work through this book you will discover to your amazement that any thought of not being artistic is only there because no one ever really showed you how easy it is to allow yourself to be creative.

Being creative is the act of expressing emotion. This can be done in many different ways. Singing a song. Writing a book. Composing a poem. They are all expressions of emotion. And so is woodcarving. If you have never effectively expressed your emotions in art, which may be because you have never had the opportunity, or because you never thought you could, or any one of a hundred reasons, which don't really matter, then you have never exposed your true creative ability. It remains latent within you.

In the final chapter of this book there is an amazing example of a highly competent carver who carved the emotions she felt without even knowing she was doing it. This person had not realized, until she gave permission for the example to be written into this book, that for years she had expressed her true emotions through the art she did. She knew what she liked, and didn't like, but until now she wasn't aware that her creativity was an expression of her emotion.

Logic has it then that if you have emotions, you can be creative, provided you are shown how. That is the inspiration for this book, what this book is all about. We will look at different kinds of carving, including whittling, relief carving, pierced-relief carving, and carving in the round, also called sculpture. We will also take a look at some of the other skills you will develop—basic drawing, some facility in photographing carvings, and the ability to observe the things you should know about anatomy for carving. All in all, if you follow the chapters from beginning to end, you will have a fun journey ahead of you.

Chapter One

EASY ELEGANCE
Introduction to Whittling

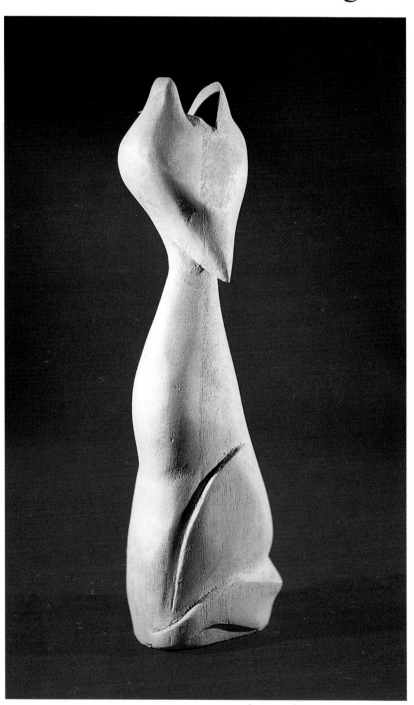

From the outset, there is one most important rule about woodcarving that cannot be stressed too much. This rule must dominate everything you do. It is a very easy one to adapt to, however, and will not cause any anguish at all. On the surface, it might seem somewhat simplistic, although it is nonetheless of great and profound importance: The only rule for woodcarving is that you must be comfortable.

THERE ARE NO OTHER RULES

You should be comfortable both in the physical sense and with what you are doing in the mental sense.

This book will give you many things to consider, many principles that you may wish to adopt to one extent or another, but it will never be dogmatic. The creation of art is about the application of choices.

If this chapter is the wrong starting point for you, you will feel uncomfortable with it. Read through the book and find an alternative beginning. The only thing asked of you is that you remember that if you get stuck and find you can't do something, or your fear barrier gets in the way, then maybe the answer lies in an earlier chapter that you have passed over.

You must be comfortable with the way you stand or sit, hold a tool, and push it through the wood, and comfortable with the results you are creating.

When you are comfortable you are relaxed, and when you are relaxed you can learn without fear, and your creativity will be nurtured without your even knowing it.

YOUR FIRST CUT—WHAT YOU NEED

In this chapter we will use a knife and some sandpaper to create an elegant fox. Carving with a knife is called whittling; and, while it is our starting point, it certainly is not the least attractive kind of carving. The author's first carving was done in 1961 with his grandfather's penknife, pictured beside it in **1-1**.

To make our fox, all you need is a piece of wood— American poplar or basswood, stone pine, white beech, yellow pine, all equally adequate—and a good knife. (See Appendix 4 for a complete listing of the common and botanical names of all woods mentioned in the text). Finishing the surface will be done with materials all available from the local hardware store.

Choosing a Knife

For your knife, it is important to choose one that both is comfortable in your hand and has a reasonable length blade—one that is not too short and stubby, nor too long and cumbersome. Trial and error is the best testing method, so if you can borrow a knife or two to try out, then do so.

1-1 *This little bust of Queen Nefertiti is about 4 inches high. It was the author's first carving and was carved, with the penknife shown, from Australian red cedar (Thuja spp.). It is finished with sandpaper, shellac, and wax.*

The handle is the most important part affecting your sense of comfort. Clearly one that is flat with sharp edges, or is too short for your hand, will be uncomfortable for you to use. Many knives are not made with a specific task in mind, and have blade and handle shapes that are uncomfortable and impractical for particular purposes.

The steel in the blade is important too, from the points of view of both ease of sharpening and the length of time it will stay sharp. The latter is called "holding an edge." Preferably the blade will stay sharp for a reasonable period of time so that you are not constantly frustrated by a blunt tool. Unfortunately, it is just about impossible to tell how good the steel is without using it for a length of time. The safest, although not always the most reliable, method is to buy a blade with a reputable brand name.

Avoid purchasing a knife for general whittling that has a wide blade. It will be too awkward to create small shapes. This is not to say it can't be done, just that it will be harder.

Some different configurations of knives and blades are shown in **1-2**. On the left are two blades that are good shapes for whittling, although the shorter one may be just a little too short for easy use in common situations. The penknife is the wooden-handled one shown in **1-1**, and this style of blade may be a little too wide for most common whittling situations; similarly the one with the round handle may be too wide. The preferred blade has been inserted into a standard chisel handle on the far right. While this handle may look a little bulky and awkward, it is well worth trying from a comfort point of view.

Sharpening Your Knife

Tool sharpening is a learned skill; a significant part of the sharpening process is the determination of the most appropriate shape of the bevel.

The principles you will learn for knife sharpening are also transferable to chisel sharpening. The main difference is that for a knife there is most often a bevel on both faces (sides) of the blade; for a chisel there is mostly (not always) a bevel on one face only.

For making the fox in this chapter and for all the carving in this book, the most appropriate configuration for your knife is a bevel on both faces of the blade. This enables the blade to be used just as easily each way up.

The preferred shapes of the bevels for your knife are shown in **1-3**. These bevels are achieved by sharpening the knife on a flat bench stone like the one in **1-4**.

A flat bench stone is designed for sharpening flat tools like knives and carpenter's chisels. It is inappropriate for curved woodcarving tools, as we will see in later chapters. The stone must be kept clean from dried oil and metal filings. Wash it in warm soapy water, or soak

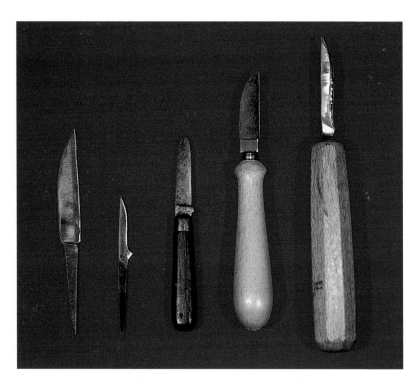

1-2 The wider blade will be too awkward for most whittling; a thicker handle may prove to be a lot more comfortable than a thinner one. Too long a blade will be just as difficult as too short a blade. Choose one that is about 2 inches long and about ¼ inch wide. The thickness of the steel in the blade is also important. If it is too thin, the blade will bend under pressure because it will not be strong enough, and too thick will make it difficult to sharpen. Choose one that is about ¹/₁₆ inch thick.

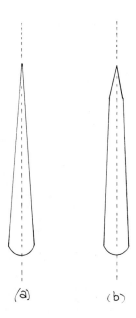

1-3 Make the bevels flat on both sides of the knife. A blade that is the ideal thinness is shown on the left in (a). The thicker the steel in the blade, the wider the bevels will have to be to create a thin cutting edge. Only by trial and error can you get it right. If the blade is too thick and the bevels are too narrow, then it will be difficult to push the knife through the wood. The most likely cause is that the bevel angle is too high, like the one shown in (b).

1-4 Keep the sharpening stone clean so that it will cut efficiently. Hold the knife fairly flat on the stone, otherwise the bevel angle will be too high and the tool will be too hard to use. Lubricate the stone with light machine oil. Choose an "oil stone" that has a very fine surface—too coarse, and it will scratch the knife blade. Neat's-foot oil (a leather preservative) is also a preferred lubricant. It clogs the stone less, doesn't irritate the skin, and the steel particles float away from the cutting edge as you grind.

it in mineral turpentine if it is particularly soiled. A clogged stone will not cut the steel, and if it is covered in metal particles from previous sharpening sessions, these will scratch and possibly chip the cutting edge of the knife.

Choosing the Wood

We have chosen poplar because it is light to hold, soft and therefore easy to cut, and not stringy and pulpy like some woods that are also light and soft. Poplar has a pleasant neutral color and is not too grainy. Radiata pine, Western red cedar, Douglas fir, and Oregon sugar pine are all examples of softer woods that can be whittled relatively easily. Radiata pine is tougher than the others and of the four would be a last choice (1-5).

Is Your Wood Suitable for Whittling?

There is a simple test you can do with a knife to help decide if the wood you have access to is suitable for whittling.

With a sharp knife, the wood should be easy to cut and cut cleanly without splintering. Sometimes you will be cutting against the grain; so, if at first some splintering occurs, then try in the opposite direction to see whether it cuts cleanly.

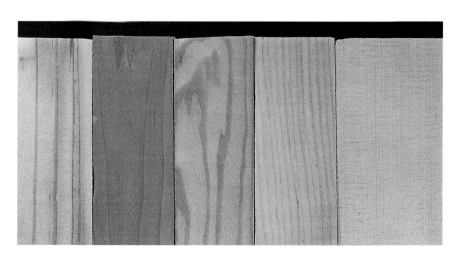

1-5 From left to right, the woods are Radiata pine, Western red cedar, Douglas fir, Oregon sugar pine, and Eastern white pine, also known as Quebec yellow pine. See Appendix 4 for the botanical names of wood.

Holding Your Knife

Safety and comfort are the two most important issues. If you hold your knife correctly, there is no reason why you should ever cut yourself. A dangerous method for holding a whittling knife is shown in **1-6**. The chances of cutting your thumb are obviously very high, and it is also often very difficult to maintain accurate cutting with this method.

The correct way to hold your knife, using both hands and pushing the knife away from you, is shown in **1-7**. Try using this method a little while so that it becomes comfortable and does not feel awkward. It will not always be possible to use this method, as there will be cutting situations where holding the knife differently will be more appropriate; however, for the majority of situations this is the preferred method.

1-6 DO NOT hold your knife like this—the risk of injury is too high. Your knife should be held as shown in 1-7.

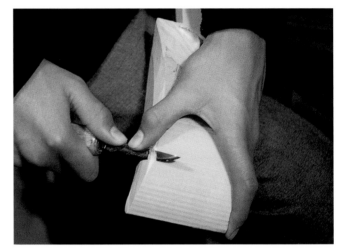

1-7 Hold your knife in one hand, and push it away from you with the thumb of the other. Once you have used this technique for a short while it will feel very comfortable and natural, and it is perfectly safe.

1-8 It is imperative that you find a comfortable posture. Not only does it make whittling easier, but it also improves safety and reduces fatigue.

It is important to find a comfortable posture; some experimentation may be necessary. Try sitting on a stool, resting your forearms on your thighs, and tucking your elbows into your sides—this may help overall control (**1-8**). Finding a comfortable posture for carving is always the first thing you should be aware of; it will help you avoid getting tired and improve safety.

Getting Set Up

The design we are going to carve is the stylized fox shown in **1-9**. Some alternative patterns you could choose from are in **1-10** and **1-11**. These slightly longer patterns might be good to try after following through with our fox. For the elongated cat in **1-11**, you can have a go at drawing your own side profiles.

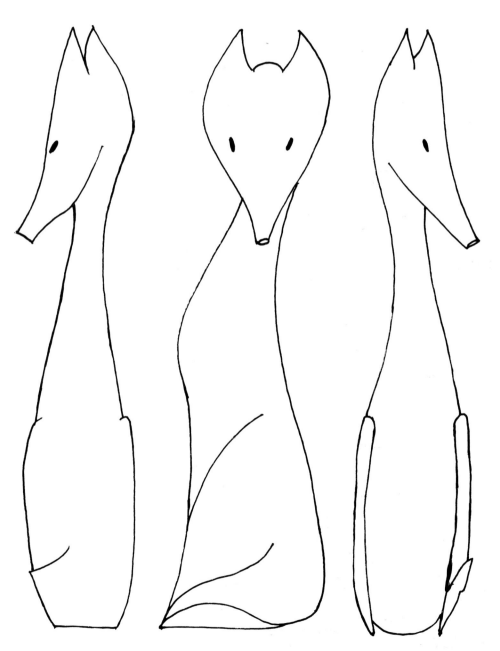

1-9 Increase this pattern on a photocopy machine by about 125 percent. Transfer the outlines of the front, sides, and back of the fox onto the wood using carbonized paper, the grid method, or freehand. Commercially purchased wood measuring 2 inches thick in its undressed (rough-sawn) state will be approximately 1⅝ inches thick when dressed (machined smooth). So if you start with an offcut from a dressed nominal 2 × 6 board 12 inches long, it will be satisfactory for this carving.

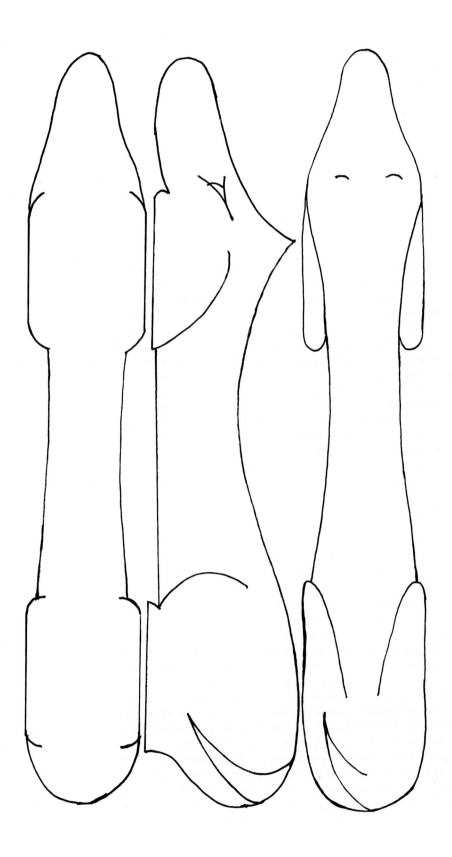

1-10 *Here's a friendly pooch you could use as an alternative or additional pattern when enlarged by about 125 percent. As with the fox pattern, you can also use the design by transferring it to the wood freehand or with the grid method.*

If you enlarge the drawings in **1-9** on a photocopy machine by about 125 percent, the fox design will comfortably fit on a piece of wood measuring 1⅝ inches × 2 inches × 10 inches long. After enlarging the pattern, trace it onto some see-through tracing paper; then use some carbonized or graphite paper to transfer the pattern to the wood. Alternatively, draw it freehand if you feel comfortable doing that;.You might also try the grid method: draw a grid pattern on the drawings in **1-9** directly on the book and draw a corresponding

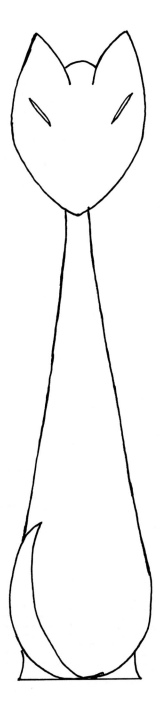

1-11 Try developing your own side profiles for this elongated cat. You will need to enlarge this pattern by about 140 percent, draw freehand, or use the grid method.

1-12 Make sure the patterns are the right way around—it is easy to mistakenly reverse the front and the back, for example! Cut each pattern out, and tape it to the wood so you can see how the design "works."

grid pattern on the wood. Then transfer the outlines freehand onto the grid on the wood (you can see the grid method illustrated in Chapter 5, "Dreaming of Drawing?" in illustration **5-8**). Before you have actually transferred the pattern to the wood, you might find it helpful to use one set of enlarged photocopies of the drawings to check the layout by cutting them out, and taping them in place on your wood. Then you will be able to see how the pattern works in relation to the block. You can clearly see the areas that need to be whittled away, and you can see how the profiles relate to one another front to back and side to side (**1-12**). If you own or have access to a band saw or a scroll saw you could now cut the profiles along the outlines, saving a little time in the carving process, although this is not necessary (**1-13**).

1-13 Here we can see how the front and side profiles match up. In essence, it is necessary to remove the square corners and all the flat surfaces so the fox is "round." The profiles front to back and side to side will always remain the same, no matter what the shape is in between—that is, whether it is round or flat, the outline of each view stays the same.

NOW, YOU ARE READY TO GET STARTED!

Follow the carving sequence shown in the illustrations, shaping the larger curves first (1-14). It is important with all the projects throughout this book to work out a general carving sequence before starting. A good principle to follow is to create the form first and decorate it second. If we apply this concept to our fox, we will achieve the basic body and head shapes first, and then set about decorating it with the ears, eyes, legs, and tail. Cut away the front and back waste and the wood between the ears, leaving the snout attached completely to the neck. (1-15, 1-16).

1-14 Commence whittling by removing the sharp corners of the block. Use your bench hook, and press the top of the block up against the back cleat to hold it still. Alternatively, whittle as shown in 1-8.

1-15 Once you have removed the top corner, carve away the drawing of the face, down to the side profile. The face will have to be drawn back on when you are ready to cut the side profile.

1-16 Here the back profile is cut away, before starting on the sides, which will require cutting on the legs.

1-17 With the tip of your knife, mark in the top of the thighs. You can see in this illustration to the left of the thumb that the face has also been redrawn in place, and some whittling has been done around the chin area.

1-18 Finish shaping the body and head, drawing on the profiles as needed. This can easily be done freehand.

1-19 This is the back view of 1-16. You can see the cutting in of the leg has just started.

Once you have created the basic form of the fox, it is necessary to redraw the detail for the decoration—that is, the ears, eyes, legs, and tail.

Mark the lines in with your pen or pencil, and cut them in with the tip of your knife (1-17). If you are happy with both where they are and how they look, then leave them alone. Fiddling with them is sometimes a dangerous thing to do, as more often than not we cut away too much in the wrong place and permanently damage our work.

It is this decoration that gives character to the fox, in the same way as the shape of the corners of the lips on a face, or the wrinkles on the skin, give expression. These decorations are often very subtle, and very little needs to be cut away to make them look one way or another. It is best to remove only small amounts at a time, in case you want to alter the direction of a curve to give a different "look." Finish shaping the body and head, drawing on the profiles as needed (1-18, 1-19). You can draw the profiles on freehand.

About Sandpaper

Sandpaper can be very useful and also very destructive. Sandpaper is one of those things that are often seen as a quick fix, but it can cause more trouble than it is sometimes worth, because it is misunderstood.

Sandpaper is made from grit adhered to a paper or cloth backing, which is sometimes waterproof so that the paper can be used with a lubricant that washes the waste material away to keep it clean. This is called "wet and dry" paper.

The grit used varies depending on the material to be sanded. For example it may be aluminum oxide, glass, silicone carbide, diamond dust, garnet, sand, or other "cutting compounds." For raw wood, aluminum oxide (generally white) is very effective.

Sandpaper grinds the surface of the wood and does not cut through it like a sharp knife does. Steel wool, which is made up of ribbons of finely cut steel, has a cutting action rather than a grinding action. Steel wool may also be used very effectively for fine finishing of wood.

Because sandpaper grinds the surface away, it has a dulling or rounding effect. If you sand a surface covered with facets as it might be from a gouge, the paper will round off the ridges, softening them accordingly (1-20).

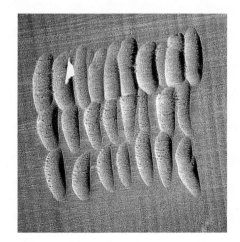

1-20 On the top half of this piece of white beech, the surface is covered with shallow dishes formed by a series of cuts with a gouge. On the bottom half, they have been sanded with some aluminum oxide paper, which has removed the ridges.

These abrasives will all have a similar effect on the surface of raw wood. They will scratch the surface of the cell walls and, depending on the nature of these cells, will damage them by grinding and tearing them. If the size of the grit on the paper is too large, this damage will be visible to the naked eye, and may be serious enough so that it can only be removed by recutting the surface with chisels or other tools. Sanding along the grain will reduce the visibility of damage.

As our fox is not "realistic" in the sense of being accurate in anatomic detail for a fox, there is a danger in making any of the subsequent decoration of it too sophisticated. Keep the eyes to slits, and don't try to make the legs look like real ones. We are looking more for the suggestion of eyes, legs, and tail rather than exacting detail.

It is not absolutely essential that both legs be identical in shape and size. In the case of our fox, fairly close is good enough (**1-21**, **1-22**, and **1-23**). This may sound casual; however, as we will see in later chapters there is no symmetry in nature and there are few straight lines. Details on the left side, for example, rarely match details on the right. In fact, we will see later

 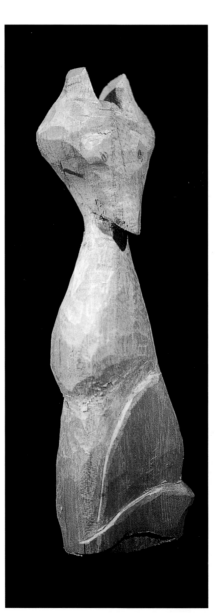 

1-21, 1-22, 1-23 Cut out the ears, and set in the tail and thighs. Rotate your fox, and you will be able to follow how the tail and legs work. Keep referring back to the original drawings, and you will easily visualize how it all fits together. Keep your work as tidy as possible, as it makes the finishing process much easier and faster. Cut in around the chin.

in Chapter 13, "Let's Face It," that if we duplicate shapes left and right, we create a look that can sometimes be grotesque and unnatural. Keep working from place to place, until you have the overall shape and appearance that you are looking for in comparison to your pattern (**1-24**).

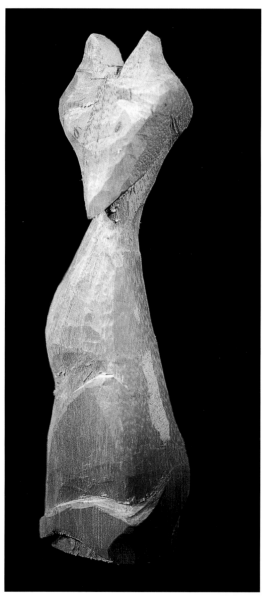

1-24 Keep working to get the shape as you want, but don't worry about symmetry or realism for your fox.

Important Note on Sanding

Sanding is not a satisfactory substitute for removing material with hand tools. A common failing is that the carver does not go far enough with the carving activity, but rather tends to stop short of completing the chisel work, choosing to complete the shaping with sandpaper. This is not a particularly satisfactory shaping method, as the end result tends to be a rounding off of the carved shape, rather than significant substance removal. For example, rough surfaces may end up smoother, but they will most likely end up an undulating series of bumps rather than the desired smooth and flat surface. Sanding is a satisfactory method for material removal only where the slightest reshaping is needed, and where a hand tool is inappropriate.

Sanding will also alter the surface texture (because it grinds the external walls of the wood cells), and this will alter the nature of the reflected light, which in turn may alter the wood's color, making it look lighter.

It is also important to note that most sandpapers leave a residual amount of grit behind in the pores of the wood, and this grit will be very damaging to the sharp edge on your tools. If it is necessary to use a tool in the wood after sanding, carefully brush or vacuum the surface first to remove any particles that may be left behind.

The size of the particles of the sanding grit is given a number by the manufacturer. This number reflects the diameter of the particles. The higher the number, the finer the grit. For wood, an 80 grit (or lower number) can cause significant scratching that may be difficult to remove. For most woods, 120 is about as low a number to go without causing damage. Sand with this first, then progressively move to higher numbers until the desired finish is achieved.

For your fox, purchase a sheet of 120, a sheet of 240, and a sheet of 400 grit. The numbers are printed on the reverse side.

Because sanding rounds the surface off, be careful not to round off the edges of the legs too much or around the eyes, making your work less effective.

FINISHING

Once you are happy with the general look of your little fox, it is time to "finish" it. In this case, we will complete our carving by treating the surface with sandpaper, and then applying a sealer and some wax. See illustrations **1-25**, **1-26**, and **1-27**.

About Sealers

There are as many wood finishes as there are ideas. However, there are some principles that apply no matter what finish is used.

First, wood surfaces that are not sealed will collect house dust, particularly if they are carved. When a surface is shaped by a knife or chisel, the cells of the wood near the surface are cut through, exposing an open cell vessel to the atmosphere. These vessels will collect dust, and the wood will eventually take on a gray hue. Sealing these open cell ends will prevent this from happening.

Further, the smoother a surface is, the better it will allow surface finishes to perform to their specification. If you require a mirror finish from a varnish for example, this can only be achieved if all the pores in the wood are filled and sealed off in the first place. A wood sealer can also act as a grain filler, helping to create a perfectly smooth surface. Some sealers are not designed to be fillers but just sealers; so check the manufacturer's specifications to be sure your intended use of the sealer is appropriate.

The pores or open cell ends in our piece of yellow pine are very small, so a sealer that is not a filler as well is adequate.

Brush on a commercially available sealer available from your hardware store. This sealer would normally be a clear liquid and will dry in a short time.

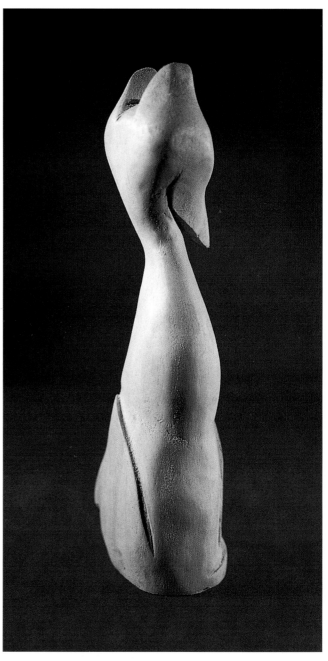

1-25 (above), 1-26 and 1-27 (opposite) Once your fox is sanded smooth or to a texture of your liking, apply some furniture wax. There are many different waxes available from suppliers; some can be applied directly to raw wood like your fox. Check the manufacturer's instructions for best results.

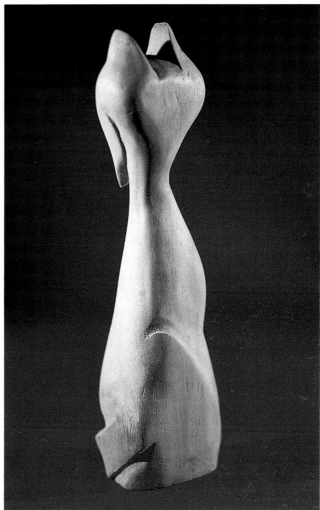

About Waxes

Finally, we need to apply some wax to our fox, to give the wood a low sheen, which will enhance its appearance and make the surface smooth and pleasant to touch. A regular furniture wax is sufficient; this can be purchased from your supermarket. It will most likely be made from beeswax, which is made from the bee's honeycomb. The wax will have a solvent to make it soft enough to apply; this will evaporate reasonably quickly, so the surface can be polished without too much delay. Read the manufacturer's instructions for applying the wax. Be careful not to apply too much at once, as it will dry to a sticky, lumpy surface, and will be difficult to smooth over. Several very thin applications take very little time, and will give an attractive sheen, whereas one overdose may cause a lot of frustration.

It may be necessary to reapply the wax to refresh the surface; however, this is infrequently needed. When the wax is dry, buff it with a soft cloth that will not leave lint behind.

Chapter Two

KIDDING AROUND
Introduction to Carving

At some time or other just about everybody who ever has contact with kids wants to make something for them. More often than not we don't have the tools or we find the practicalities of making toys too daunting. In this chapter, we will introduce the woodcarving gouge, use our knife again, and see how easy and not too time consuming it is to make some fun toys.

HAVE FUN MAKING SOMETHING FOR A KID

The patterns for an owl, duck, and bear that you could use to make a child's mobile or a fun child's toy are given in **2-1**, **2-2**, and **2-3**. Each carving will use the same carving tools, and we will start to explore different ways of holding our work in progress. The pattens are full size and the wood should be proportioned accordingly.

This style of carving is known as *carving in the round*, obviously because it is three-dimensional. In the next chapter we look at *relief carving*, which is used mostly for flat panels and furniture; in later chapters we look at *pierced-relief carving* and other kinds of carving in the round, often also called *sculpture*.

2-1 Use this drawing of an owl, or the others of a duck or bear, in the same way as you did for your fox. With a little bit of imagination, it is a simple matter to draw your own profiles for the side view and even the back view. If you do have a go at drawing these profiles, make sure you have each profile lining up with the matching height and width as appropriate.

2-2 A duck is a favorite item among young children. The drawing of the duck is used in the same way as you did for your fox in chapter one. Use your imagination, to draw your own profiles for the front view and the top view. If you do want to use this design, make sure you have each profile lining up with matching height and width as appropriate.

2-3 For this bear, the side profile is shown as well as the front, for your convenience since this is the pattern we will use to get started carving in the round. This is actually a slightly more complicated pattern than the owl or the duck, so all of the instructions and details in this chapter apply equally well to using the other patterns.

CHOOSING YOUR WOODCARVING CHISELS

There are many hundreds of woodcarving tools of all sorts of shapes and sizes (see also Appendix 3 for a discussion of the basic tools we will use for the projects in each chapter). At first, the array can be quite confusing; however, once one realizes that there are a few basic shapes and the rest are variations on the theme, then common sense takes over. As we progress through the various chapters, we will introduce the different kinds.

The first advice, however, is to avoid buying predetermined sets of tools. Most manufacturers put together "beginner's sets," and for the most part they are quite reasonably selected; however, as you develop your own style and tool preferences, you will most likely find that some of the tools in your original set you rarely use. This is because we all develop our individual ways of doing the same thing, and what might be one person's choice may be quite different to another. Further, the set we originally purchased might be best used for carving in the round, and, if the preference turns out to be for relief carving, then several more tools may need to be purchased.

The best thing to do is to buy tools individually as you need them and build up your personal set on the basis of what you need when you need it rather than what someone else thinks you should have before you are ready.

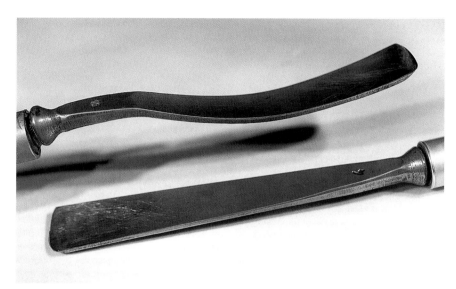

2-4 *The size of a woodcarving tool is determined by the distance in a straight line between its shoulders. This is a ⅞-inch (20mm) gouge. The manufacturer will allocate a number to the shape of the curve, so that each tool can be distinguished from the other. This is a No. 3 curve from a particular manufacturer. The tool on the bottom is known as a No. 3, ⅞. The one on the top is "long bent," and has a prefix L, so this is called an L3, ⅞. Some manufacturers use a numbering system developed in England in the nineteenth century, called the Sheffield List; however, not all manufacturers use this list, so each brand tends to be different.*

In this chapter the chisels we will use are a gouge, a V tool, a fluter, and a skew. They will all be standard sizes, and they will each be tools you will use for all kinds of carving.

The Gouge

The *gouge* is the basic woodcarving *chisel*. While historically all the different styles of carving tool have a name, today they are generically referred to simply as chisels.

A good basic, workhorse gouge for either carving in the round or in relief is one that has a slight curve on it and is about ¾ inch (20mm) across. Gouges also come in a *long bent* form, and these are particularly useful if there is a great depth to the carving (**2-4** and **2-5**).

All woodcarving chisels have a *bevel* on them. It is the angle and shape of the bevel that dictates the behavior of the tool. The bevel shape is the result of the grinding and sharpening process. Understanding the simple theory of the bevel allows you to sharpen the tool to the most efficient shape for the work you want to do. (See below and Appendix 2 for information about tool sharpening.)

The V Tool

The *V tool* is also known as the *parting tool*. It is used for cutting grooves for decorations such as feathers, cross-hatching, and lines of all sorts, and it is also used in the starting process for relief carving. Refer to Chapter 3, "What a Relief!"

This tool looks a bit daunting as far as sharpening is concerned; however, it is relatively simple. Treat it as you would a regular gouge, rolling it over the apex as described in the sidebar below and in Appendix 2, where we look at many of the specific questions that frequently come up about tool sharpening.

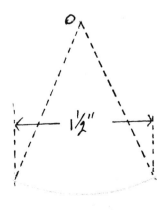

2-5 *Be careful not to fall for the trap that all tools with the same curve number have the same curve, because they don't! The No. 3, for example, will refer to all of the manufacturer's tools that form a particular arc, and the ½-inch size, for example, will refer to the measurement between the shoulders in a straight line (not all manufacturers use the same arcs).*

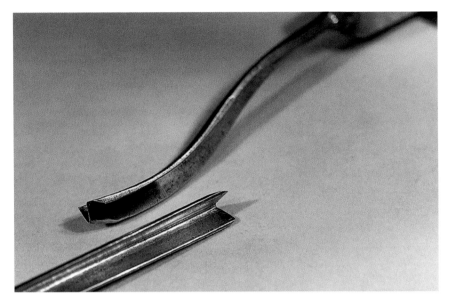

2-6 *Two V tools, a medium-sized (¼-inch to ⅜-inch) and a smaller (⅛-inch to ¼-inch) tool, are the most the average carver will ever need. Larger tools may be needed for large sculpture. V tools also come in straight and long-bent styles.*

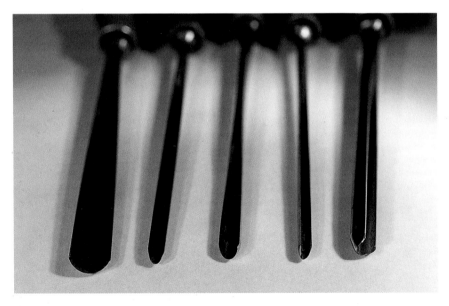

2-7 *Sharpening the fluter requires care, particularly for the smaller sizes. It is very easy to grind away too much from the bottom of the curve, and make a hole in it. This is similar to the problems that can arise with overzealous sharpening of a V tool.*

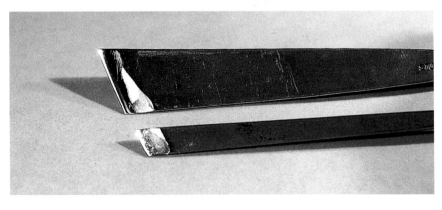

2-8 *A larger skew is often easier to handle than a smaller one, although the smaller one may seem easier in the beginning. When you sharpen the skew, ensure the bevel is not too convex itself, otherwise the tool is too difficult to get to cut. It keeps wanting to slip off. See Appendix 2 for more on sharpening.*

Choose a V tool that is about ¼ inch (6mm) across the shoulders. This is a good average size, and will suit most work. V tools used for deeper carving also come in the long bent form similar to the gouge (2-6).

The Fluter

The fluter could be described as a high-sided gouge. Shapes of the cutting edge will vary from deep "U" to more circular curves (2-7). Use the fluter for deeper decorative grooves around eyes, under wings, and for hollowing out the ears in the patterns. Choose a medium to small size, say ⅛ inch (3mm), for general use to start with. Eventually several larger sizes may become part of the tool kit. A very small fluter ¹⁄₁₆ inch (2 mm) or less is a handy substitute for a V tool.

Always be careful using smaller fluters not to put too much pressure on the blade, otherwise it might bend, particularly at the top of the shaft near the handle. These tools would not normally be used with a mallet. This caution applies to most small tools, particularly where the cross section of the tool is square or round.

Some tools have a rectangular cross section, with the narrow edge across the top, making them less likely to bend under downward pressure.

The Skew

The skew is one of the most useful of the carver's tools, one of the easiest to sharpen, but often one of the most difficult to master. It has a bevel on both sides, making it easy to flip over to reverse the cutting direction. It is the only carver's chisel that enables the carver to create any shape of convex curve. A gouge also can be used upside down; however, the shape of the concave curve for which this is possible is limited, decreasing the flexibility of the gouge for convex curve making.

Choose a skew that is larger than you think is actually necessary or comfortable. A ⅞-inch (20mm) skew is easier to handle than a ¼-inch (6mm) skew, and although both may take a little while to master, in the end the larger one is more often the preferred size. The skew is seen in **2-8**, and holding it is demonstrated in **2-9** and **2-10**.

2-9 and *2-10* Control is the most important issue with the handling of the skew. Resting your wrist on the work and holding the elbow high to get the angle of approach right will help. The skew is essentially a paring tool; however, it can be used as a knife and is handy for getting into tight corners.

SHARPENING YOUR NEW TOOLS

If at all possible, purchase tools that come ready sharpened, or at least ground ready for sharpening. Your tool supplier should know whether the tools are "ready" or not. Some manufacturers prepare their product for immediate use, so there is little if any sharpening required to get started.

Most modern tools will stay sharp ("keep their edge") for reasonable periods in softer woods. In the event that you cannot buy presharpened tools, it is quite possible the tools will need to be shaped by grinding before they can be sharpened and used effectively for your carving.

Three Stages of Sharpening

There are three basic stages to a complete sharpening. The first is the *grinding process*, during which the bevel on the tool is shaped in the most appropriate way for the wood to be carved. Preground tools are normally shaped for softer woods, which is perfect for the carvings in this book.

The second is the *sharpening process*, during which the cutting edge is finely tuned and scratches are removed from the bevel. This is performed with the slip stone as shown in **2-11** and **2-12**.

The third is the *honing process*, during which the cutting edge is polished to bring the cutting blade a fine, razorlike edge.

The Sharpening Process

After the first stage of sharpening where the bevel on the tool is shaped in the *grinding process*, the cutting edge is finely tuned in the *sharpening process*. Ensure the stone is clean from dried oil and steel particles from previous sharpening sessions. A clogged and dirty stone will not cut effectively, if at all.

Rock the tool on its curve, and move the stone around the tool in a circular fashion (**2-11**). This gives greater control than moving the tool around the stone. Hold the stone at an angle so that it lies flat on the bevel, otherwise all you will do is grind off the sharp edge, and make the tool blunter (**2-12**).

Continue the process putting light pressure on the stone so that you can feel it "biting" into the steel cutting its surface. Use a lubricant such as mineral machine oil, or more traditionally the leather preservative neat's-foot oil. This oil will not clog the stone quite as much, will not irritate your skin, and has a surface tension that causes the fine ground-off steel particles to float away from the cutting edge as it is being sharpened, so you are not grinding steel on steel.

2-11 *Make sure you hold the slip stone and the tool so you can see the bevel lying on the stone.*

2-12 *Do not hold the skew at too high an angle, otherwise you will round off the end of the tool and make it more blunt.*

Once a slight burr is felt on the upper side of the tool, stop this process. The burr is steel that has been "rolled" over the edge. It will easily break away. If you continuing once a burr is achieved, all you will be doing is unnecessarily removing steel. Now move to the third stage of the process, which is *honing* using your strop.

To sharpen the tools you need to complete the carvings in this chapter, you will need the small slip stone, some lubricating oil, and a strop as shown in **2-13** and **2-14**. Follow through the description for the sharpening process and the honing process in the sidebars. Answers to frequently asked questions about tool sharpening can be found in Appendix 2. These sharpening tools are also shown in Appendix 2 as well as in Appendix 3 on the essential tools needed for the projects. Keep the stone and the strop clean so they will cut efficiently.

There are many questions that arise as we undertake woodcarving, ranging from questions on the nature and use of wood itself (see Appendix 1) to the nature and use of our tools. Perhaps the most common question from us all is, "How long will this tool stay sharp?" and the best answer is, "It depends"—on the nature of the steel it is made from, the shape of its bevel, the hardness of the wood, and what you do with it in the wood. On the surface this is not much of an answer, but within it there lie a number of very important issues that will be covered as we progress.

The Honing Process

The strop shown in **2-13** is made from ⅛-inch belly hide pinned to a backboard of ½-inch-thick ply. Use a firm leather; one that is too soft will simply wrap around the tool and round off the edges you are trying to sharpen. Stropping is the process of honing the tool edge. It is a polishing process that removes all the scratches from the bevel and brings to the cutting blade a fine, razorlike edge.

To speed up and make the stropping process more efficient, apply a metal cutting compound to the leather surface. You could use 600-grit (or finer) silicon carbide powder or aluminum oxide powder. More commonly available would be equally effective metal-polishing compounds such as motor vehicle exterior chrome polish, or engine-valve grinding paste.

2-13 Draw the tool at the angle of the bevel with the bevel facing down on the leather strop, Then turn the tool over to ensure there is no residual burr.

With the bevel facing down on the leather strop, draw the tool along the leather at the same angle as the bevel (**2-13**). Do this action until the bevel is polished. Be careful not to hold the tool higher than the angle of the bevel (**2-14**).

Turn the tool over and repeat the action on the topside. It is not necessary to polish the

2-14 Do not hold the tool at a higher angle than that of the bevel, otherwise all you will do is round off the sharp end and make it blunt again.

whole of this surface, but it is necessary to ensure there is no residual burr at the cutting edge and that it is polished. The tool should now cut through the wood with a smooth action, with very little resistance; there should be no scratch marks or tearing showing on the surface of the wood.

HOLDING DEVICES

To undertake these carvings, we need to look at some different holding devices. It is necessary to carefully consider how you are going to hold your carvings, first from a safety point of view and second from a practical, "doing it" point of view.

There are many and varied types of holding device on the market. Some work a lot better than others for certain applications, and the only way to effectively assess these devices to your satisfaction is to use them. For most woodcarvers, a homemade device offers a very satisfactory solution to many holding situations, and, of course, the price is right! We will use homemade devices in this chapter.

Offcut material from other projects is often the best source of small amounts of wood for holding devices for carvings; leftover screws and dowels are also very handy. The astute carver will save these sorts of material for future use.

Metal vises are of course also useful; however, great care must be taken not to hit the tool end on the metal, because some very severe damage may be done to the tool. Just one slip can effectively end the carving life of a chisel. You could put a facing of wood (thick ply is excellent) in the jaws of a vise as a lining to help protect your tools.

Holding the Carving—Safely

For safety, the most important issue is to avoid wherever possible holding the carving in one hand and the chisel in the other. It is inevitable that sooner or later you will severely cut your hand. A sharp tool can cause considerable permanent damage.

For all holding devices that you will ever use, it is important to consider your personal comfort. If your holding method uses a board as a base under the work, for example, ensure that the clamps holding the board to the table or benchtop are sufficiently far apart so they don't get in the way of your hands or tools. Allow yourself room to move comfortably, and place the handles of the clamps downward so you do not hit your eyes or head on them as you move about.

You can use newspaper sandwiched between the carving and a board at the base to hold your work steady, as shown in **2-15**. This will not work particularly well for higher carvings like our bear, unless the footprint (outline of the bottom) is large enough to create a good glue area.

2-15 Ensure that the board attached to the base of the carving is thick enough so it will not flex after clamping to the bench—⅜ inch (10mm) thick is adequate. Screws that are too short may pull out. For these carvings, 1½ inch (40mm) is adequate. If you ever use the paper and glue method (illustrated) suitable for flatter carvings, use only a water-soluble glue, such as a PVA (polyvinyl-acetate) type. To remove the carving, push a spatula into the cardboard and it will break away. Remove any remaining cardboard by soaking with water. Water will not damage the carving.

2-16 *A board is attached to the base of a carving using two screws to stop the carving from rotating under pressure from tools. To form the correct holes to accommodate screws, three drill bits are used: a countersink bit to make the cone-shaped hole for the head of the wood screw; plus one size of twist drill the same diameter as the shaft of the screw (the part of the screw without the thread below the head)—use this for making the hole in the baseboard; and, a third bit, slightly smaller than the diameter of the thread of the screw. Use this for making the hole in the base of the carving.*

Another simple system is shown in **2-16**: a board is used as a base with the carving screwed to it, and then the whole thing clamped to a benchtop with G clamps. A general-purpose device called a bench hook is shown in **2-17**. This can be made from offcuts from another project. Over time it will be likely you will want two or three different sizes of this device, as you

will discover just how versatile this simple tool is. We will use it to rest our carving on, enabling us to get started with the roughing-out phase.

The extra wood left on the bottom of the bear can be cut off when the carving is finished, or left there as a base. It is inappropriate to insert a screw into the legs of the bear, as we will be carving away much of the material between them.

LIGHTING

As we progress throughout the book, we will look at different lighting situations, particularly in Chapter 3. As a general principle, lighting that creates shadows is the most effective for woodcarving. Fluorescent lighting is not appropriate because it is designed to be shadowless, whereas cross lighting from a reading light creates good shadows and is by far the most flexible and readily available in most households.

Natural sunlight provides excellent cross lighting; however, it doesn't stand still for long enough! Halogen (and to a lesser extent, tungsten) lighting will provide the cleanest light for carving; many modern reading lights use the halogen technology. A floor pedestal light will offer the greatest flexibility for moving the light around the work. Lighting for shadow creation is more

2-17 *A handy size for a bench hook uses an offcut board about 8 inches (200mm) wide, and cleats made from a 2-inch by 1-inch (50mm by 25mm) strip. Use a reasonably firm, soft wood such as Radiata pine. Timbers such as Western red cedar are generally too soft and will damage too easily, although the bench hook is "disposable" once it is well worn. Use clamps and glue to attach the cleats rather than nails or screws. Nails will eventually pull out and screws will work loose.*

critical for relief carving than for carving in the round, so for this chapter anything other than fluorescent light will be adequate.

Whichever system you use, ensure the lighting is adequate to comfortably see by. This may seem rather obvious; however, if you have not done this kind of activity before, some experimentation may be necessary. In addition, new activities such as wood-

Nominal Dimensions: Rough-Sawn vs. Dressed Wood

Wood that is sold by a lineal or cubic measurement will be either *rough-sawn* or *dressed*. If it is rough sawn, it may be cut to a specified size; for example, a board may be sold as being "one inch thick." If it is oversized, it is sold as a "full one inch," and it may be even more than one-quarter of an inch larger. This custom will vary from country to country.

If the wood is dressed, this means that it has been machine planed to clean off the rough surfaces. It will be planed from the rough measurement to the new and, obviously, smaller dressed measurement. The rough measurement is typically used to classify the wood, becoming the *nominal dimension*. The actual dressed dimension will vary from one market to another, typically on the scale of a region or country; thus it is important to be familiar with the dressed dimensions for your region. Wood dressed from stock that is one inch thick may end up as small as ¾ inch thick. Thus, a nominal 1 × 2 could have a surfaced dimension of ¾ inch by 1½ inch.

Before ordering wood, therefore, first not only check the correct way of describing the measurements for the wood for your region, but also make sure of the correct local interpretation of those measurements. Your lumber merchant will help you.

carving also expose shortcomings that we may not have noticed before, and one of these is the quality of our eyesight. If you feel there is eyestrain at all, first check the adequacy of your lighting, following which it may be necessary to visit your optometrist for an eye check. For those of us already wearing glasses, it is quite possible that the lens correction is inadequate for the work we are about to undertake.

GETTING STARTED

We will carve the bear from 1-3, which is the most complicated of the three designs. Everything covered in this example can be applied to the other patterns.

Buying Your Wood

Wood is normally sold or purchased by weight, lineal, or cubic measurement. The nomenclature will vary from country to country; however, in the majority of cases it will be either an imperial (pounds, feet, inches, etc.) or a metric measurement. See the sidebar for things to watch out for when buying dimensioned lumber. Wood sold by weight is normally unseasoned and in a log, lump, or block. Wood suitable for a sculpture, therefore, will most likely be for sale by weight. It will also most likely be unseasoned, and the carver needs to take this into consideration during the planning stages.

Wood can certainly be carved wet, but wet wood is much heavier than seasoned wood (because it contains more water), and it may be necessary to take this into consideration as well. Wet wood is also a lot softer than dry wood; hard woods that are still fairly wet can be more easily worked than the same wood dry.

TRANSFERRING THE PATTERN

Prepare the wood and transfer the pattern in the same manner as for the fox in Chapter 1. If there is anything about the pattern that you would like to change, now is the time! Your satisfaction with the design you will carve is the most important thing about it.

Before you anchor the bear to the baseboard, use your gouge to cut as closely as you can to the profile lines holding the block of wood up against the cleat on the bench hook. This is a perfectly safe operation, provided you hold the wood behind where you are cutting with the gouge. If you wish, you could use your knife in the same way as you did with your fox in Chapter 1. Alternatively, you could cut to the profiles with your scroll saw or band saw, as has been done in **2-18**. Keep the offcut pieces that are shown in this illustration as templates for redrawing the profiles as necessary. The finished cutout is shown in **2-19**.

Don't try to cut too deeply at any one time, as the tool may get stuck in the wood. If this happens, *do not lever it* to remove it, because you might break the tool. Instead, move the handle sideways, and the gouge will easily fall out of the wood. Many smaller cuts are a lot better than fewer larger ones. If you find the height of the cleat you are resting your carving on is inadequate, screw an extra layer on. Similarly, if the bottom cleat is not high enough, the bench hook will slip off the bench. Again, add another layer to correct this.

It is important to take plenty of time to get used to how the tools feel in your hand and how the wood reacts to them. Do not rush anything.

Try using the gouge upside down as well as the "correct" way, which is with the bevel pointing downward to the wood. When it is used upside down you will notice the tool tends to nosedive into the wood. This is because there is no bevel against the surface of the wood. It is the bevel that pushes the tool back up and out of the wood. The rounder the bevel is, the greater this tendency, and the flatter

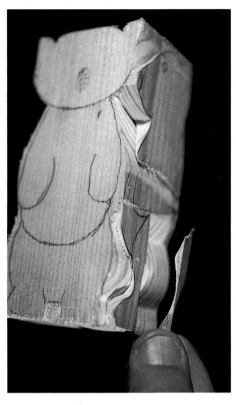

2-18 Remove as much waste wood as you can before attaching the bear to the base. If you have access to a band saw, you could cut the profile of the bear out as shown in the front and back views on the left of the illustration. It is important to remember that with all carving or sculpting in the round, irrespective of the direction of the view, the perimeter or profile of the object is the same in the reverse 180-degree view. It is the parts inside the profile that will vary from view to opposite view. If you cut a profile with a band saw it is best to make sure it is a "square-on" side, front, or back view you are cutting. This means that the profiles are at right angles to one another, otherwise it will be too difficult to interpret what you have cut. Keep the offcuts as handy templates. Once you have cut off one side, you will have to redraw on it the profile for the front.

2-19 Before you anchor the bear to your baseboard, you may wish to remove the corners of the bear's head, and do some basic roughing out in the tummy area. Some shaping can be done around the legs and feet, being careful not to accidentally cut them off. If you do, simply glue them back on with fast-setting glue. Glue them back on right away, before the wood fibers become too disturbed and misplaced. As you can see, the bear is very square-edged and flat-surfaced at this stage. The most important carving principle at this point is that wherever there is a square edge or a flat surface it must be made round.

the less the tendency. If the bevel is ground "hollow," that is, concave, it will also nosedive into the wood, and it will not work. The shape of the bevel dictates the behavior of the tool. (See also Appendix 2.)

Once your carving looks like that in **2-20**, it is time to attach the base to a board. Make sure the screw is firmly seated home and there is no gap between the bottom of the bear and the baseboard. Some notes on preparing holes for screws were seen earlier in **2-16**. It is important that the preparation for securing the wood for carving is thorough, as there is nothing more irritating than the wood moving around while you are trying to shape it. Clamp the baseboard firmly to your workbench or table with two G clamps (refer to Appendix 3), and you are ready to proceed. Ensure the handles of the clamps are pointing downward, so you do not hit your face on them.

2-20 Once your bear looks something like this, it is ready to be mounted at the base to a board.

A Note on Repairing Accidents

Every woodcarver will have accidental breaks from time to time. There are many things that can be done to avoid them, and these we will cover progressively. In the meantime, the best practice to follow is to repair damage immediately. The less interference that happens to individual cells and fibers, the better.

Carefully work some fast-setting glue into the grain on both parts. Gently massage the two pieces back together so the fibers fit back together the way they were. Tape the break with some tape that does not have a permanent adhesive, and allow it to set.

If you use a rapid-setting cyanoacrylate (CA) adhesive (superglue) you should be able to recommence carving almost immediately. Use glue that does not have a residual color. Some glues dry gray or milky white. Check the manufacturer's instructions and, if no one can assure you how it dries, test it first on some scrap wood.

CARVING SEQUENCE

The carving is shown sequentially in progress from different angles in **2-20** to **2-38**. Study the illustrations carefully, noting the changes between each one. At first the photos might appear to be like a massive blur and altogether too much information; however, if you take your time, assess the differences, and compare them to your own carving as you progress, you will become very comfortable with them.

Place some scrap wood under the ends of the clamps so they do not dig into the underside of the tabletop, or into the baseboard if you don't want to damage it. Your bench or table must be firm and not likely to wobble under pressure. In later carvings we will use a woodcarver's mallet; this will increase the pressure on the table or bench and, therefore, the likelihood of movement.

There are no rules as to the best place to start or the right order of proceedings; however, the following principles will greatly assist you:

Work around the carving constantly. Avoid carving too much on one side or in one place, as it is too easy to get things out of proportion. You may find that you have carved away too much on one side and have not left enough for the carving to remain "round." See the sidebar in case of accidents.

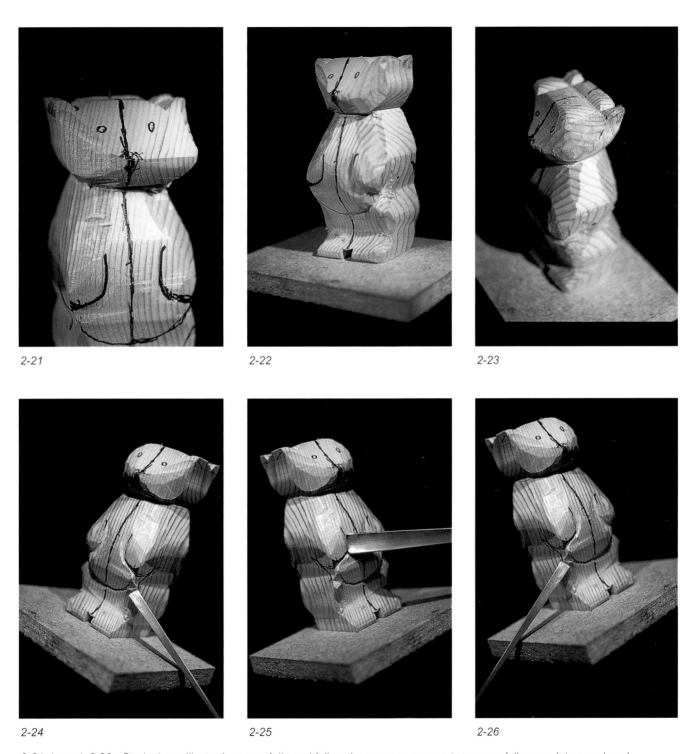

2-21

2-22

2-23

2-24

2-25

2-26

2-21 through *2-26* *Study these illustrations carefully and follow the same sequence to successfully complete your bear!*

2-27

Identify focal points or focal lines, and make sure these are in the right place. Mark them on the wood. These become those parts of the carving that all the shaping moves up to or away from.

Choose a focal area as a place to start, such as the top of the bear's head—or its nose.

Approach the piece in its entirety as you progress through various stages of carving; you should avoid any tendency to work on one part, such as the head, to completion before you move on to the body, for instance. It is better to fine-tune the entire carving as a whole. This way, the parts flow together better, and they end up "belonging" to one another.

Remember on our nature subject there are no flat areas, no sharp edges, and no corners of any kind. If you have one, you know it has to go.

2-28

2-29

2-27 *through* **2-32** *Continue carving as you study the sequence and notice the details that differ from image to image.*

A Note on Copy Carving

Copying someone else's work is not the easiest thing in the world to do. In fact, to make an exact copy of anything is very, very difficult. With all the carvings in this book it is important, therefore, to be perfectly at ease with the limitations of your copying expertise and, indeed, not try too hard. Use the illustrations as a guide; interpret them as best you can and as much or as little as you want. Unless you specifically want to try, do not attempt to religiously copy them. It may take you too long, it may become frustrating, and you may lose interest.

It is often more fun and a lot more interesting to leave your own stamp of individuality on your work. You will naturally develop your own style, which further reduces the perceived need to copy every detail. Indeed, you might not even like what the other person has done.

Sometimes copying a particular style or pattern is an excellent way to learn a particular technique. If this is your objective, then copy as exactly as you wish. Otherwise, use other people's work for inspiration and ideas, and apply your own interpretation to it.

2-30

2-31

2-32

SURFACE FINISHING

When you have your bear about the same as the one in **2-33**, **2-34**, and **2-35**, it is time to decide the kind of finish you want.

As with many things, the best way to understand surface finishing is to experiment with it. There are some basic principles, though, that will apply no matter what you decide:

Dust is one of the worst enemies of your finished carving. The open pores in the wood will collect house dust very quickly and turn the surface gray. If you look at carvings in many very old cathedrals and churches, they often have a gray tinge that cannot easily, if ever, be removed. It is important to seal the surface to stop dust penetration, even if you want to leave the surface finish natural. There are a number of clear surface sealers available at retail stores that can be brushed on; they do not leave any residual color or sheen. They can also be the base or undercoat for other finishes.

For many carvings, the glossier the finish the less attractive it might be. This is because a gloss surface reflects light, and a carved surface that has many convex and concave curves on it will reflect light in many directions. This reflection can often interfere so much with the appearance that it makes the carving look cheap and unattractive. Woodcarvings often respond best visually to a low-sheen waxy finish than a synthetic "plastic" look. If you have any doubt, test different finishes before you apply anything to your work.

The application of a surface finish may swell some of the fibers and cell walls and make the surface feel rough. This is particularly the case with spirit- and water-based liquids. Once dry, it may be necessary to wipe over with a very, very fine sandpaper (600 or 1000 grit) or a super-fine steel wool (0000 grade).

Whichever surface finish you finally elect to have, it is also important to ensure the wood is not covered with scratches from sandpaper or steel wool. These will show and spoil the end result.

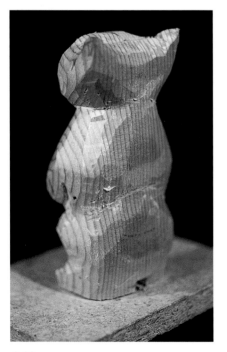

2-33

2-34

2-35

2-33 through 2-35 When you are ready, sand your bear to the desired finish. You may want to leave some texture on it to give it a natural look.

For your bear, in order to keep it "natural looking," treat it first with a clear liquid sealer that you can purchase in your local hardware store. Sometimes they are called "sanding sealers." Danish Oil™ (a trademarked product manufactured under license in different countries) can also be used as a sealer. Once the sealer is dry, the surface might feel a little rough. This is because the solvent in the sealer has swollen the grain of the wood and raised it. Wipe it over with a very fine paper (e.g., 1000 grit) to remove the roughness.

Once sealed, a light application or two of a beeswax furniture polish (from your local supermarket), and you have a natural-looking finish like the one in **2-36**, **2-37**, and **2-37**. This finish will last a considerable time before it needs to be freshened up.

Apply furniture wax sparingly with each coat. If you use too much at a time, the wax will dry thick and possibly lumpy and will not be easy to polish. Several very thin applications is a lot faster to bring to a pleasant sheen than one thick one.

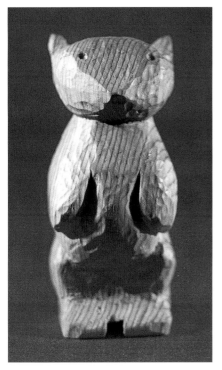  

2-36   2-37   2-38

2-36 through 2-38   Use a clear liquid wood sealer before applying wax. Wax and polish the bear, screw in an eyelet; now all you have to do is make the owl and the duck to complete your mobile!

Chapter Three

WHAT A RELIEF!

Relief Carving

In this chapter we will make our first relief carving, combined with some simple carving in the round. We will make a nut bowl you can use at your next dinner party. Before we commence our bowl, there are some key things that we need to know that will help make our carving activity easier and more successful.

There are different kinds of relief carving, broadly broken into different categories. There is high relief (where the carved shape rises above the background to a depth one-half its apparent circumference) and low relief (where the carving is raised from the background such that none of it is actually detached from it, such as a coin). Medium relief is in between; pierced relief is where the pattern is cut through from one side to the other and relief carving is done on both sides, such as a screen or a music stand.

SELECTING WOOD

Woods that are commonly used for serving food include those that do not taint the food flavor with perfume oils or resins. Some of these are Asian kauri, teak, and Baltic pine. We will use Eastern white pine (*Pinus strobus*), which goes by many other names, including Canadian or Quebec yellow pine.

CREATING A DESIGN

The origins of the pattern for our nut bowl are shown in **3-1**. These are two leaves from the common domestic geranium plant. A small leaf has been placed inside the larger one to create the idea for a two-level nut bowl. The bowl will be carved from one piece of wood, with the top leaf forming the relief part of the

Notes on Recycled Wood

Using recycled wood is a favorite for the environmentally conscious woodcarver, and old timbers are frequently better quality than new wood of the same species, particularly when compared to modern plantation growth. Plantation-grown wood is often grown faster than in its natural "wild" state, and is sometimes more pulpy and stringy. If there is a choice between the two, the "free range" tree normally produces better wood for carving purposes. It is very important to check recycled wood for screws and nails, which will cause significant damage to tools.

Sources of wood for recycling are commonly building demolition sites and old furniture components. One source often overlooked is old solid-core doors, which may produce low-density boards such as jelutong, which was used as the core usually underneath plywood or veneer, which forms the visible outer surface. Check out that ugly old door before turning your back on it—there might be hidden treasure inside!

3-1 Two leaves in different sizes are placed with the smaller leaf in the center of the larger leaf to create an interesting concept for a carving. The object will be carved from a single piece of wood and serve a practical purpose as a two-level nut bowl. The bowl will really be a combination of high relief in the center and carving in the round.

carving. This bowl will really be a combination of high relief and carving in the round. The leaves are sketched in a full-sized top view in **3-2**. The views of the leaves from the front and the back in **3-3** are shown in relation to the top view. The top view shows the positioning of the two leaves relative to one another in what is called *plan view*, and the front and back views give a sense of the three-dimensional configuration by showing what are called *elevations*. This is an important drawing technique, which is covered in Chapter 5, "Dreaming of Drawing?" It is easy to do; all it needs is a bit of practice. It is important to make sure everything corresponds by drawing straight reference lines that align the prominent features from one view to another.

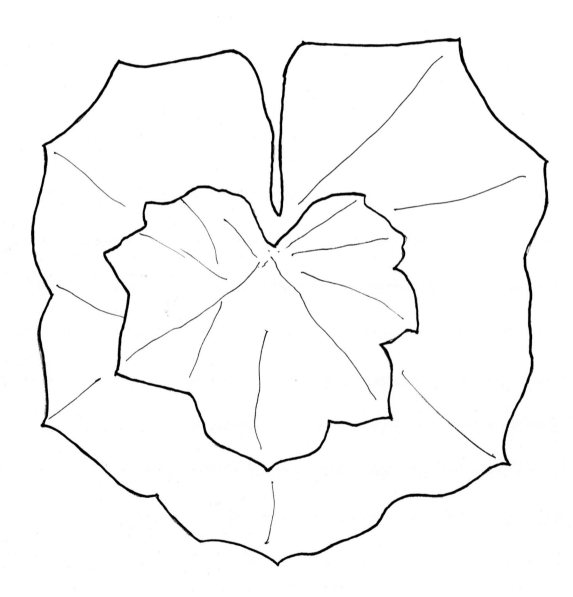

3-2 This is a full-sized drawing of 3-1. You can use this top view as a pattern on your wood for carving. Transfer the top profile to the wood and use the sketches of the front and back views in 3-3 to see the three-dimensional relationship of the two leaves.

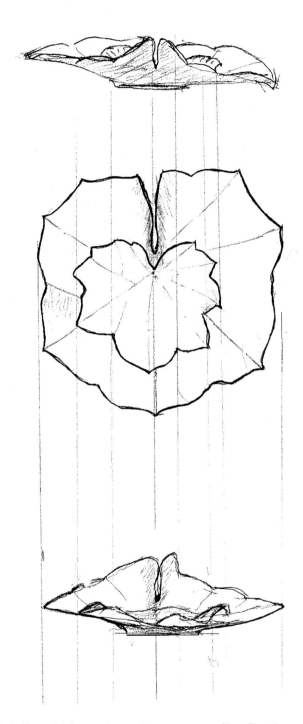

3-3 Draw the leaves to create your own profiles. Practice this kind of drawing and you can use it to make all kinds of records for future carvings. The leaves or flowers will shrink and die, but your drawing will be available forever.

Tools for Carving the Bowl

See Appendix 3, "Essential Tools for the Projects & How to Hold Them," for the basic tools you will need. For carving this bowl, we also want to have these two gouges:

> ½-inch, almost flat gouge
>
> ¼-inch, almost flat gouge

You might also find it useful to have a ½-inch, long bent gouge at hand, but this is optional.

GETTING STARTED MAKING THE BOWL

To make a convenient-sized bowl from our drawing, use a piece of Eastern white pine measuring 6 inches square and 2 inches thick (150mm square and 50mm thick). It can be rough sawn, as we are going to carve away the surface. If the wood is smooth on the surface, however, this does make it easier to transfer the drawing to it. We will start by transferring the pattern to the wood and cutting out the basic top-view profile. But before we start carving, we will want to think through how we are going to go about carving the piece.

Transferring the Design to the Wood

Trace the drawing onto some translucent tracing paper that you can buy from your local art supply store. Transfer it to the wood using some carbonized paper, also purchased from the art supplier. If you are unable to obtain carbon paper, use the grid method: draw a grid pattern on the drawings in **3-2** directly on the book or on a photocopy and draw a corresponding grid pattern on the wood. Mark the points on the grid on the wood where the pattern lines cross the grid lines on the drawing. Then you can complete the pattern on the wood by sketching freehand from point to point. onto the grid on the wood (you can see the grid method illustrated in Chapter 5, "Dreaming of Drawing?" in illustration **5-8**).

Mark the sides of the wood as well, with the elevations front and back.

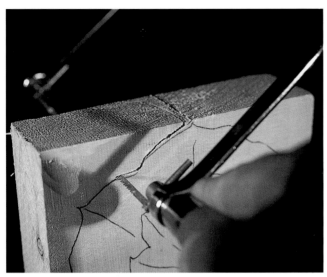

3-4 *Hold the block firmly in a vise, use a sharp blade, and take your time. If you do not cut precisely on the line it will not matter as the edge is meant to be irregular.*

3-5 *The area of the base that touches the tabletop needs to be large enough to keep the bowl stable, but not so large as to make the bowl look ungainly. About a third of the diameter should be adequate for both, with the flat area just touching where the fissure in the leaf ends.*

Cutting Out the Profile

Once the top-view profile is drawn on, cut it out with a scroll saw or a coping saw as shown in **3-4**. The wood is fairly soft, so cutting by hand will not present a problem with this thickness, especially if a new, sharp blade is used.

THINKING AHEAD BEFORE CARVING

We must now consider the order of carving—here we need to consider the logic of where to start. But first— how are we going to secure the bowl to the workbench so we can carve it safely? The easiest approach for a piece of this size and shape is to screw the base to a board, and clamp that to the workbench.

Once the top is carved, it will be impossible to turn it upside down, and carve the bottom without breaking the top, as it is an uneven layered surface. Logic has it, then, that we should carve the bottom before the top. The area of the base that should be left flat is sketched on the bottom of the wood, as shown in **3-5**.

CARVING SEQUENCE

Now follow the carving sequence in illustrations **3-6** to **3-25** to complete your bowl.

To start working on the wood blank, stop the workpiece up against the edge of your bench hook so that you will be able to easily use the 1-inch (25mm) gouge to remove the waste to form the base (**3-6**). But first mark the shape of the sides of the leaf all around your bowl blank before you start carving away the waste. This means you will have two boundary lines, one representing the boundary of the waste to be removed from the bottom, the other representing the boundary of the waste to be removed from the top.

The area to be carved away is marked with diagonal parallel lines, both on the bottom and the top, as shown in **3-7** and **3-8**. This shading or hatching is a convenient way to continually remind yourself what should be cut away and what should be left.

Use your gouge to cut in a curve down to an even depth first. The slope of the sides of the bowl will be reasonably the same all around. Then you will need to carve away the remainder of the waste down to the required levels.

3-6 Stop the bowl blank against the edge of your bench hook. You can use your 1-inch (25mm) gouge to remove the waste, but if you have a long bent almost flat gouge, you may find it easier to cut. Cut in a curve down to an even depth first.

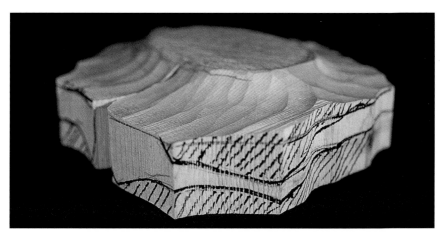

3-7 After carving down to a common level, bring the carving down to lines that mark the shape ot the sides. Mark the area to be carved away with diagonal parallel lines, on both the bottom and the top, not marking in the area that should remain uncarved.

3-8 The shape of the sides of the leaf should be marked all around your bowl blank. This means you will have two lines, one representing the boundary of the waste to be removed from the bottom, the other representing the boundary of the waste to be removed from the top. Bring the edge to a blunt overturn, which will not chip, rather than to a sharp point.

3-9 With the waste removed to bring the bottom to its boundary line, the block is ready to be attached to a board. Then it can be securely held while the top is carved.

Once you have removed the bottom waste marked by the diagonal lines, the underside of your bowl will look like the piece in **3-9**. Only the waste not yet removed from the top is left to be carved away. It is now the time to anchor the base of the bowl to a board, with two screws, in the same manner as the little bear in Chapter 2, "Kidding Around."

Start to carve the top by cutting a groove with your V tool around the top pattern, as in **3-10**. This only needs to be about ¹⁄₁₆ of an inch deep. Use this groove as a guide for making a series of vertical incisions with your 1-inch gouge. These incisions need to just barely overlap each other, as shown in **3-11**, otherwise you are wasting your effort making them overlap too much. Have the bevel of the gouge pointing toward the

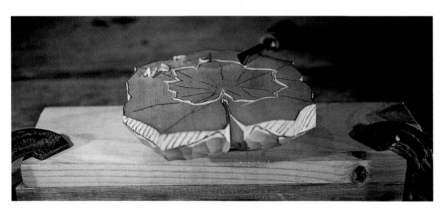

3-10 The carving of the top is begun by cutting a shallow groove around the inner leaf outline. The ¹⁄₁₆ inch deep grove is cut with the V tool to act as a guide for making vertical incisions with the 1-inch gouge.

About the Atmosphere

For the woodcarver, the prevailing atmospheric conditions have special significance, apart from the effects of atmosphere on wood generally.

It is important to note that a carved surface has significantly more exposed surface area than a flat surface. This means that the atmospheric conditions may have a greater impact than otherwise might be the case. A large panel will be more inclined to warp after it is carved than before. The carved surface will lose or take up moisture faster than a plain flat one, and may continually have a different moisture content than the reverse side of the wood.

A carved surface may be inclined to check (crack) more than a blank one, and it may well dry out during the carving process, and make it more difficult to carve. The surface may become more brittle and chip easily, or become more stringy, depending on the nature of the wood. If this is the case, spraying with a fine mist of water from an atomizer will make a considerable difference to its "workability."

pattern, so the tool will of its own accord move away from it. You end up with an edge sloping outward from the pattern. It will be necessary later to cut this edge in vertically, as shown in **3-12**. Once you have made these sloping cuts all the way around, cut back in the opposite direction, with the bevel pointing down, and clear out the waste. Repeat this procedure as necessary to cut down to the required depth.

To cut the edge in vertically, it is necessary to push the tool down into the wood with the bevel also vertical, as in **3-12**, otherwise it will push outward and make a sloping cut. To hold the bevel vertical it is necessary to slope the tool outward (or back toward you). You may need a mallet or your body weight to push the gouge into the wood at this angle.

3-11 The gouge starts in the shallow groove with the bevel pointing toward the pattern. The tool naturally moves away, leaving a sloping cut, with each successive cut just overlapping the last. After the sloping cuts go all the way around, the edge is cut down vertically to clear out the waste to the required depth.

About Concave Curves

The carving of the concave curve generally presents some special challenges when the curve is particularly deep and/or tight, as might be the case with bowl or spoon carving. There are two positions during the carving of these curves that may be problematical, and where the choice of wood may affect the outcome. The first is where the tool may be pushed up the concave slope and into the end of the grain. Most woods do not want to be cut against the grain and will either break or tear away.

The second is at the bottom of the curve, where the two sides meet. There is of course no such place in the geometry because it is a continuous curve; however, in the reality of carving, cleaning out the bottom can be tricky. Do not try to cut a continuous curve from one side to the other if the curve is tight, as you will almost certainly encounter the first problem. Rather, where the downward cuts meet from either side of the bowl, clean this off with a tool that is as close as possible to the curve of the bowl, and cut across at 90 degrees to the direction of the previous cuts. It is very easy to dig a trench across the bottom and score it unintentionally, so great care is needed.

3-12 The edge is cut down vertically by holding the tool outward from the work so that the bevel is vertical as the tool is pushed into the wood. You may need to lean your weight into the cut or use a mallet to push the gouge at this angle.

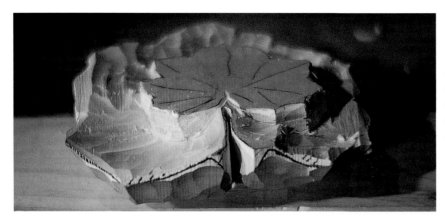

3-13 As you carve the vertical perimeter around the edge of the top leaf, you will start to see how the leaf bowl takes shape. Naturally let yourself start to put some curve into the bowl as you carve. Carve down to a depth of about ⅝ inch.

Now that the bowl is the right way up, proceed to cut in (i.e., expose) the top leaf, as shown in **3-13**. With the bevel toward the pattern, place it in the groove, and if necessary use your mallet to carve away the material down to the depth line previously drawn in place. Once again, carve to a vertical perimeter around the edge of the top leaf. Carve down to a depth of about ⅝ of an inch. As you start to put some curve into the bowl, see the sidebars on concave and convex curves. Let your natural creative instincts take over, and some natural shapes will emerge!

In the carving out process you may discover previously hidden featrures of the wood, as seen in **3-14**. Being the natural medium that it is, wood can have many surprises. What we see here is a hidden branch that was growing inside the main wood. Branches start to grow right at the center or pith of the host branch or trunk, and like this one are often undetectable unless they are visible on the outside of the piece of wood. If you are lucky, the feature can be carved around or removed entirely, as it can in this example. It can be carved away, so it will not interfere with the bowl.

3-14 This shows something that cannot be easily foreseen and at times may be a frustration. It is a hidden branch that was growing inside the main wood. Fortunately in this case, the little new branch is in an area that is to be carved away, so it will not interfere with our bowl.

3-15 You can see by looking closely that the grain around the branch curves tightly in toward it. This bent grain is very likely to be brittle and difficult to carve. Make sure your gouge is very sharp, and cut around the branch; you should be able to pull it out without causing any damage.

The best way to proceed is to carve carefully, cutting around the hidden feature to understand in what direction the grain is going (**3-15**). The grain around the branch curves tightly in toward it. This is the result of the branch's growing through the growth rings and forcing the wood aside to make room for it. This bent grain is very likely to be brittle and difficult to carve, and will break away if you are not careful with it. Use a gouge that is very sharp to cut around the branch, and you should be able to pull it out without causing any damage.

Continue with your carving and shaping of the leaves. Notice in **3-16** that things look like they are getting to be a bit of a mess. To avoid this, keep your tool sharp, and clean up as you go, keeping things tidy. Otherwise, on a larger scale carving the cleanup you will need to do may be quite substantial. It is easier in the long run to keep things tidy as you go. On the far left of the illustration, on the bottom leaf, you can see some straight lines in the wood where it has broken as the tool has been pushed across it. If this happens a lot, change the direction of the cutting until you find one that allows the tool to cut cleanly. Stringy cuts like this may also indicate a blunt tool.

About Convex Curves

Convex curves do not present anything like the potential challenges of concave curves. Generally they will be cut with a skew chisel. The skew is the simplest of all tools; its relative ease of use creating the desired curve in the chosen wood will be tempered only by the shape of its bevel. For maximum ease, do not try to cut the convex curves up the slope (because you will be cutting against the grain), but rather down or across.

A bevel on the skew that is too round will make the tool slide off a small-diameter convex curve because it will be too hard to control. However, this rounder bevel may be an advantage with harder woods, so some experimentation might be needed. There will have to be some compromise among the curve of the bevel, the curve being carved, and the nature of the grain of the wood.

3-16 The messy look of the bowl at this stage is largely due to not keeping the carving cleaned up and possibly working with a tool that has become too blunt. Become aware of the signs that will alert you that you need to sharpen your tool. It is easier in the long run to keep things tidy as you go.

3-17 You can start to undercut the edge of the top leaf as you shape your bowl, and after you have a vertical edge all around the perimeter of the top leaf. Keep the undercutting somewhat irregular as you use your gouge with the bevel facing upward to cut about ⅛ inch above the background and down toward it, followed with a horizontal cut along the background. The undercutting should reach about ¾ inch underneath the top leaf.

3-18 After undercutting the top leaf, clean up the work. Check that the undercutting is sufficient and the bowl deep enough to allow the intended contents of nuts and olives to sit comfortably.

3-19 This is the side view of the undercutting. It is probably a good idea at this stage to shape out the dish of the top leaf before refining the shape of the undercutting any further.

As you shape your bowl, and after you have a vertical edge all around the perimeter of the top leaf, you can start to undercut it (3-17). With the bevel upward, first make a cut about ⅛ of an inch above the background and down toward it. Then make a horizontal cut along the background. Repeat this until the undercutting is about ¾ inch underneath the top leaf (it should not be precisely regular, as this would make it look unnatural) and reaching up to the top edge of the top leaf, but without creating a sharp edge that might chip off.

Clean up the work you have done so far. Don't make the wall of the top leaf too thin, as it will not have enough strength for normal use (3-18). If the undercutting is not high and deep enough, you will not be able to fill it with nuts and olives. Try a few nuts in it to check. Any nut oil or moisture won't do any damage at all. The bowl at this stage is still reasonably chunky (3-19). You could refine it now, although it is probably better to shape out the dish of the top leaf first, and then adjust everything altogether.

Before you go any further, though, check that the screws in the base are still tight. Some pulling may have occurred if they were not a perfect fit. Commence carving out the dish of the top leaf using the same gouge (3-20). Don't take too much away with each cut. A little at a time is faster in the end, more accurate, and less likely to cause any unwanted damage.

About Dryness

Sometimes when a wood is seasoned to local climatic conditions it becomes very dry and brittle on the surface to be carved. This may also occur in dry climates, or during abnormally windy or dry conditions in an otherwise temperate area. If your wood has been dried in a kiln, it is also possible its cell walls have become a little more brittle than they might during air-drying. Since wood is capable of absorbing and releasing moisture from the atmosphere on a continuing basis unless it is sealed, its moisture content will vary with the prevailing weather conditions.

If the wood is crumbly and brittle, and these are not necessarily normal conditions for it, try moisturizing the surface using an atomizer pump to spray a mist over the surface. Allow it to soak in for a few minutes or more, and there should be a noticeable difference in its carving characteristic. If a wood is naturally crumbly and brittle, either carve it while it remains unseasoned, or test it to see if regular misting with water will make carving easier.

3-20 As you carve out the dish of the top leaf, start from the outside and move toward the middle. This keeps the pressure where the wood is and stops any breakage that may occur if you start cutting from the inside out.

3-21 *There may be some chipping in a grainy and soft wood such as this as you shape the inside of the top leaf. The leaf design is naturally serrated so this is not a problem as long as the chips are not big.*

3-22 *In continuing the shaping process, the gouge is being used to clean up and shape the edge of the leaves with a chamfer. This makes the edge more attractive and helps protect it from later chipping.*

Shape the inside of the top leaf as shown in **3-21**. Notice on the edge of the top leaf right above the edge of the gouge there is some chipping. This might happen with this wood, as it is reasonably grainy and soft. It will not matter as the edge is naturally serrated and is not meant to be perfectly formed; however, be careful not to create chips that are too big to be natural.

Continue the shaping process now that you have the top leaf dug out (**3-22**). Shape the edge of the leaves with a chamfer to help make the edge more attractive, and protect it from later chipping. Make the top leaf curved enough to hold some nuts, and like the bottom half, test it with some actual nuts and olives to double-check how useful it is.

Sanding & Finishing

The carving has reached the stage that it is ready to start the final cleanup with some sandpaper (**3-23**). Cloth-backed paper is best to use because it is flexible and does not break and tear like paper backing. Use a grade of grit that will not scratch the surface of the wood. In this case, a 280 grit is being used. If you are unsure which grade to use, test some different ones on an offcut, or the base of the bowl. The grade of sanding grit is usually printed on the back of the sheet; it is often simply a number 180 or 280 and so on. Commonly available grades go from 80 to 1000.

Remove the screws and release the bowl from the board (**3-24**). Plug the screws with some slivers of wood (cut some small pieces; press them in and chisel

3-23 *You can see the remains of the little branch we uncovered in **3-14** and **3-15** just to the left of the thumbnail. When you are ready to sand, use cloth-backed "sandpaper" because it is flexible and does not break or tear like paper backing. Use a grade that will not scratch the surface of the wood. In this case, a 280-grit paper is being used.*

them off) or seal the holes with some putty. This will keep water from getting into the wood and potentially staining it when you wash it. It will also stop dust and dirt from collecting.

Once you have the bowl smooth, it is time to oil the carving (**3-25**). Notice we have left the bowl surface with some of the gouge marks still showing. This helps to give the bowl a casual, natural look that would be missing if we sanded it all perfectly smooth. You can make it smooth if you wish and, if you decide you like it otherwise, cut some gouge marks back in! The remains of the branch that was uncovered can still be clearly seen. It adds an interesting decoration to the leaf, and certainly doesn't detract from it at all.

Fill up with nuts and olives, as in the photograph at the opening of this chapter, pour yourself a martini, and celebrate your very first relief carving! Enjoy!

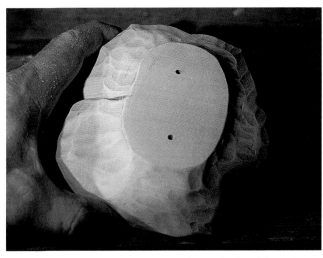

3-24 The screws are removed to release the bowl from the board attached to its back and plugged with some slivers of wood or filled with putty.

3-25 The bowl has been sanded smooth, but left with some of the gouge marks still showing to give a casual, natural look. It is ready to oil and then use. You can very clearly see the remains of the branch that was uncovered, which adds an interesting decoration to the leaf and certainly doesn't detract from it at all.

Chapter Four

NATURAL WONDERS
Found-Wood Sculpture

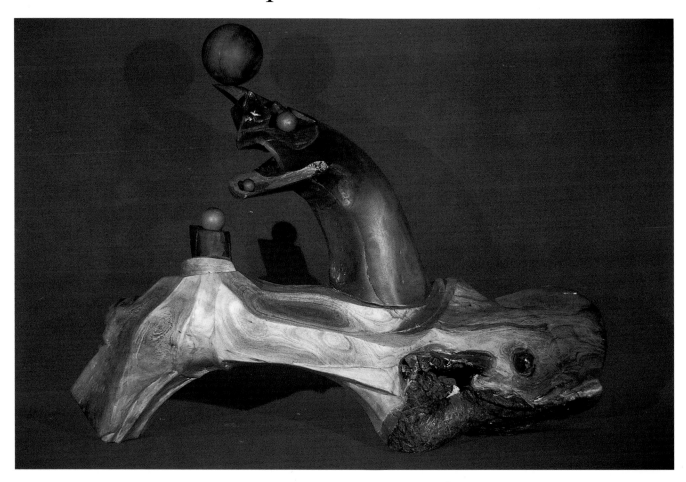

This chapter will appeal to many people who have never tried woodcarving before. It is about found-wood sculpture. "Found wood" because it is sculpture from wood that you literally find in your garden, out in the country, or in your town or city park's or garden's pruning pile! Of course, much of the end result depends on just what we find in our wood, so the more interesting our wood is in the first place the better off we will be in the long run. Trouble is, how do we know what is in our wood unless we go looking in it? And how can we choose a piece of wood that might turn out more interesting than another?

WHAT CAN WE CREATE?

The objective this natural approach to sculpture is to take your piece of found wood and see what you can find in it. All the wonderful shapes and colors of nature, packed together are right there in your piece of tree. As we move through the pages covering this fabulous new experience, we will also learn more about wood itself. We will discover more about the structure of nature's own, what we can do with it, and how we can make it work creatively for us.

The sculpture on the opposite page is one example, but it clearly depends on what we could find in our wood. The main inspiration for this sculpture is a piece of fruit cherry tree from a garden pruning. The round balls are made on a wood-turning lathe. Shape and color are the two main ingredients for successful found-wood sculpture. The discovery of both in wood is an adventure in itself, is easy and fun to do, and can create some great decorations.

Learning by Observing the Found Wood

There are many characteristics of wood that we can assess by carefully looking at a cut log or branch, or even at a tree before anything is cut. If we know the species and something about the characteristics of its wood of course this helps us identify a large number of possibilities, including color and grain patterns. By the same token, if we know absolutely nothing about our piece of wood, there is a great deal of fun to be had finding out about it, just by digging around in it!

Some of the features that we can typically observe in a piece of found wood are shown and described in **4-1**. This example illustrates what we can learn about our wood by doing almost nothing. Before we start to dig around with our tools, however, we need to check our log for dirt and sand that will inevitably ruin the cutting edge of a sharp blade. Vacuum with the household cleaner, and you will be amazed at the amount of debris you remove. Washing down with the garden hose is also an excellent cleaning method.

4-1 This is a log of an Australian inland desert wattle called gidgee. Without doing anything at all to it, an external examination of this identifies six features each of which we could use for effect in a found-wood sculpture:

There is a very rough bark, which might be good for a textured look.

On the top right-hand corner of the log, some of the bark has been torn away, revealing a light yellow sapwood underneath (the heartwood is a deep chocolate).

Below that, there is an area where some of the bark has been worn thin, revealing a pink-colored layer.

The white pointer is indicating a fissure in the log, almost hidden by the bark. This fissure could be quite deep and could be used for interesting effect.

Below that fissure is another one, also hidden in the bark,.

To the right of that the remains of a branch, just sticking out from the side. This could make a useful decorative knot.

4-2 Couldn't this privet root system become a crazy-looking spider? What else can you think of? A wandering octopus?

4-3 This root system is from driftwood found on a beach. The wood has already been washed clean and partly shaped by nature herself; with some modification to the shape to tidy it up a bit, some sanding, and an application or two of wax, you have a very imaginative creature from the deep!

4-4 These branches were driftwood and make an excellent and attractive stand for this puppet. The puppet is made from camphor laurel, which is colorful and highly aromatic.

Tree roots and branches can also be used to arrive at an interesting effect. Just imagine what you could do with the spidery tentacles of the root system from a backyard privet plant shown in **4-2**. The piece shown in **4-3** is from the root system of another but unknown tree, and some old driftwood branches became the supporting system for the puppet in **4-4**.

USING BARK EFFECTIVELY

Bark can be used for visual effect on a carving, particularly sculpture, but there are two things to look out for:

First, bark is the first place to accumulate dirt and other debris from the atmosphere, particularly if it is lumpy and open-grained bark. Sandy grit will very quickly destroy the fine edge of tools. Before using tools in bark, wash and/or vacuum out grit, hosing down if necessary. If you let the log air dry immediately, no damage will be done by plenty of water (**4-5**).

Second, bark may shrink, as it may dry at a different rate than the wood underneath it. As it seasons, it may fall off the sapwood. It is possible that with a completed carving the bark will come loose and require gluing back into place; however, it may not fit properly if the wood has shrunk more than the bark.

Tools for Found-Wood Sculpture

There are not too many requirements for this activity—just a large dose of "inquiring-mind syndrome," a vivid imagination, and a few standard tools.

See Appendix 3 for the basic tools you will need.

In the example in **4-6**, bark has been left inside some naturally occurring fissures on the outside of the small log, together with some rings of sapwood around the perimeter of the fissures. Exposed is the pink heartwood of the log, and what an attractive ornament it makes!

4-6 This is a small piece of needlewood. The natural color of the heartwood contrasts with the sapwood and the bark to produce the striking ringed effect. The fissures that form the rings are a natural part of the formation of the trunk. All that has been done is to remove the bark and the sapwood from around the rings.

4-5 Here we see dirt or "mud" from an infestation of ants. It has collected in the bark and will certainly be harboring sand and other dirt that will damage tools. It is best to remove this debris by hosing, brushing or scrubbing, and then using old chisels and knives that you don't want to pry loose remaining soil.

In our next example (**4-7** and **4-8**), the bark is left in place on one whole side of the log, and what is left makes an attractive frame that helps highlight the natural red color of the heartwood.

We can see the use of color in the wood for interesting effect in **4-9** and **4-10**. These kinds of sculpture are simple and easy to create, yet can be very effective decorations, and a lot of fun to make.

SAPWOOD

The wood underneath the bark layer is the most active within the tree for transporting the nutrients that give the tree life and growth, and is called the *sapwood*. The sapwood is often, but not always, a lighter color than the other wood, which is known as the *heartwood*. The sapwood layer can be clearly seen in **4-8** between

4-7 This is the reverse side of the small work in 4-8. Underneath this uninteresting bark is white sapwood and purple heartwood shown in the next illustration. Don't be fooled by the outside!

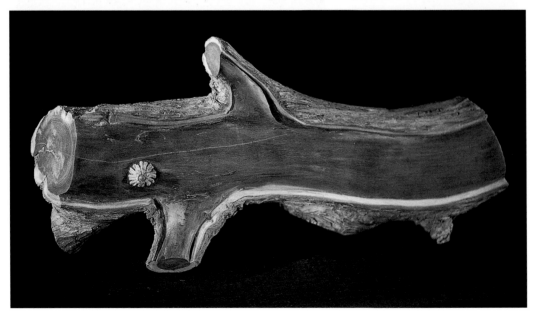

4-8 In this simple sculpture bark is removed to show the layers of sapwood and heartwood. This is a piece of "dead finish," an arid inland desert timber. The addition of the little funguslike growth made from a contrasting wood makes for a fun display.

the bark and the main body of pink heartwood. Toward the end of the growing season, the leaves typically are producing more food than the tree can use, and the unutilized food is moved radially from the inner bark and cambium toward the center of the tree. As these nutrients accumulate and break down, they eventually cause the cells to die, creating the heartwood. Thus, sapwood is characteristically carrying more moisture (water) than the heartwood, is softer (because it is younger and wetter), and is very frequently stringy and somewhat pulpy.

Its color difference makes sapwood an ideal decorative effect for many carvings; however, for intricate work or work relying heavily on shadow activity, the contrast between sapwood and heartwood may be an interference that spoils the effect. In any case, sapwood should be tested with a tool before you decide to use it in a carving, as its softer and stringy mechanical properties may render it an inappropriate choice.

When subjected to drying conditions, the sapwood will tend to contract more than the heartwood; so care must be taken to prevent cracks forming. Being relatively new wood, sapwood tends not to be as stable as heartwood. In some species the sapwood is not easily distinguishable from the heartwood, so if there is any doubt, test the wood first with a chisel.

4-9 This "bacon leg" is created by using the differences in the color of the components of the log to create the carver's intended effect.

4-10 Here a schoolchild has created his impression of an "Olympic torch" by using the different colors of American osage orange and purpleheart wood.

HEARTWOOD

The part of the tree that contains the cells that can no longer transport nutrients is called the *heartwood*. It is often, but not always, a different color and darker than the live part of the tree that forms the *sapwood*, and it is also often of greater density and more difficult to work. At the center of the heartwood is the pith, formed from the original shoot. The pith is often very soft if not rotted away, in which case the log develops a hollow pipe through it.

The heartwood is generally the most colorful part of the wood, and is normally the most desirable. Sometimes the difference in color between it and the sapwood can be used to advantage with the design of the carving. Since the outer layer of sapwood is often much less dense than the heartwood, it is important to test both with hand tools before choosing a wood for carving. If you are testing a log, be sure to dig deep enough to reach and try the heartwood.

THE SEASONING PROCESS

Carving a found-wood sculpture is often done in wet or unseasoned wood, allowing the wood to dry as the creative process progresses. It is important to understand the nature of the seasoning process, so that there is a minimal risk of damage to the carving, and the carver's ego!

Splitting & Checking

As a wet piece of wood starts to dry, it will do so from the outside inward. The cells want to shrink as they dry; they may well separate from one another, and internal *checking* (cracking) will start to appear (4-11). This can be a particularly destructive condition and greatly annoying to the woodcarver, as often there is no evidence of these internal checks until they are uncovered during the carving process. Either that, or they appear after the work is finished and make a mockery of all your hard work!

About Weathering

If you want to use your found wood sculpture outside for a garden decoration, you will need to consider the effects of weathering.

Wood contains pigments that are affected by exposure to ultraviolet light, which will fade them. Wood also contains resins and sap that will be leached from it by prolonged exposure to water. Continued exposure to water, wind, or sand (as in the case of driftwood, for example) may also wear away the softer tissues in the wood relative to the harder tissues, thereby changing its shape.

Weathered wood is silver-gray in color, may be rippled by the wearing away of some of the tissue, and may be generally softer or pulpy if all the resins are removed. As a result of weathering, carving may be made more difficult because the strength of the wood is lowered, making it less able to sustain crisp detail. The choice of weathered wood must therefore be made carefully, and will most likely be best suited to free-form sculptural purposes.

If wood is to be placed in an outdoor environment, there is little prospect that it will maintain its color and new qualities unless it is regularly treated with an ultraviolet light filter and a weatherproof surface coating. This will generally mean that it will have a synthetic glossy finish, which may not be the artist's ideal "look."

If wood is to be placed on the ground, ensure there is a moisture barrier to prevent water and fungus damage. Exposure to the highs and lows of ambient atmospheric moisture and heat may also degrade wood by causing cracking.

Checking or cracking of wood is not confined to the inside. Different factors may cause cells to part, and these include internal stresses that may be set up externally by wind or heat. There is no way of knowing of their actual existence, so for the woodcarver their discovery can be not only a surprise, but a great disappointment. Sometimes a test cut through the cross section of the log or board will reveal internal checks, which may indicate their presence elsewhere in the piece. If there is any suspicion, best to select some more wood! For some, such natural flaws are seen as unacceptable disfigurement. However, for the majority of people these characteristics can add to the overall appeal and naturalness of the finished work, particularly for sculpture. For the woodcarver who is confronted by such a distinguishing feature, it is best to maintain a philosophical outlook, considering the work as a whole, provided the feature falls in a place that does not ruin an effect (**4-11** and **4-12**).

Preventing Splitting & Checking

Do not store the carving in or near heat, wind, or direct sunlight.

If you fear the wood will dry too quickly, store it covered with a damp cloth, but watch for the development of mold.

During the carving process, if any small surface checks appear, spray with a fine atomizer mist of water to keep the surface moist. As the carving progresses, the wood will dry relatively quickly, as there is a greater exposed surface area of wood to the atmosphere when the wood is shaped than when it is in a plain board or lump.

4-11 This is an internal check that was discovered only when the wood was cut. The majority of checks are visible on the surface of the wood.

4-12 This is distortion that occurred as a result of shrinkage in this wood which has dried but did not check. This distortion can be quite dramatic and can cause considerable damage.

All woods will check if the atmospheric conditions cause rapid moisture loss. The majority of checks are visible on the surface of the wood; however, in some circumstances internal checking will occur. Checking is largely prevented by using appropriate seasoning procedures. Once wood is checked it is not normally possible to restore it. The log you find for your sculpture will most likely be unseasoned, so care will be needed as you carve it.

Effects of Wind

Wind is one of nature's most damaging elements for wood, especially because wind causes water to evaporate very quickly, having a potentially devastating effect on the wood. Rapid moisture loss from wood may cause it to shrink and crack as the cells collapse. In log form wood will split radially from the center or pith outward to the bark and also along its length. In plank or board form, wood will warp in any direction, and may also crack along and across its grain. It is important to store wood well out of wind and protected from weathering. If it is to be exposed to weather in finished carved form, make sure it is well sealed so that moisture cannot escape from it.

It must be noted that if it is stored out of the wind, this does not automatically mean that the wood will be immune from damage. The ambient atmosphere may also be very dry (that is, humidity may be very low), and there may be a similar outcome.

ANNUAL RINGS

For the found-wood sculptor, the annual growth ring can be a decorative advantage or a textural nuisance. The rings represent different growth phases of the tree, called *earlywood* or *springwood* and *latewood* or *summerwood*, as the layers correspond to the growing season. They can vary in color, density, and texture. Springwood will be generally soft, pulpy, and stringy compared to summerwood, which will generally be harder and denser. In some species, such as western red cedar, Oregon sugar pine, and Radiata pine, the growth rings alternate soft then hard, and make the timber particularly difficult to carve. In effect, the tool cuts through the softer material easily and bounces off the harder, making control awkward.

Uneven texture and irregular cutting make for a particularly displeasing carving medium. None of these

4-13 Here we can clearly see the annual rings as alternating colored rings. Also we see in the center the pith where the growth of the whole tree started. There is a stain of some kind, possibly a fungus, that is discoloring the heartwood and is visible as the darker brown blotch; there are some radial growths (new branches) coming from the center of the piece on the right-hand side; and there is some severe internal checking. This is a piece of fruit apple wood.

species are recommended for carving under "normal" circumstances (**4-13**). See also Chapter 6, "Abstract Arrangements."

CELLS

The *cell* is the basic component of wood; its characteristics determine the wood's behavior in every key area that the woodcarver will be involved with; how it seasons, how it is cut and shaped with tools, and how it takes a finish. Each species of wood is identifiable by examination of the shape, size, and layout of its cells; while this is not necessary knowledge for the woodcarver, an understanding of some of the basic behavioral characteristics of wood cells is. This understanding will help determine the best wood for a particular application. Examples of these traits are:

Soft wood with large open cells and thin weak walls is not ideal for fine detail carving, as it is not strong enough to carry it. Such large open cells are visible to the naked eye (**4-14**). Wood with larger cells will absorb color stains in large volume when the cells are cut through, and the end grain will be a significantly different (more concentrated) color than the long grain.

Blotchy, uneven color will result, unless the wood is thoroughly sealed beforehand.

Wood with long fibers will be stringy compared to that with shorter, and will be more difficult to carve than wood with shorter fibers.

Finely compacted, very dense cells will make the wood very hard and difficult to carve, and, if the cells are short as well, the wood will be brittle and crack easily. If there is no cell structure of any kind at all visible to the naked eye, the wood is most likely too difficult to work with hand tools.

The cells make up the *grain,* so if the grain is visible or there is a grainy "feel," the wood is most likely reasonable to carve.

By cutting through the end of a piece of wood with a sharp handsaw, it is possible to make some reasonable assumptions about the wood for carving. If the cell walls are weak they will tear and collapse easily, indicating the wood is potentially woolly and brittle.

There are also cells that go across the wood, and these are sometimes visible (in species such as oak) as rays that go radially from the center toward the bark. These are called *medullary rays,* and they can be an attractive feature of end grain (**4-14**).

4-14 In this piece of oak, the open ends of the cell vessels that have been cut through by the saw are visible in a wide band in the middle of the photograph. They are what look like pinpricks. The radial medullary rays are also very visible as large clusters of cells that look like light-colored lines that go across the annual rings.

4-15 Fungus is a penetrating and destructive organism for wood. It might grow on the surface of the bark and gradually penetrate the cells. Rotten wood cannot be carved since it crumbles away.

FUNGUS & DECAY

Also commonly known as mold, fungus can be a destructive organism when infesting wood **(4-15)**. Fungus generally needs moisture and warmth to grow; its presence often indicates poor storage conditions. Wood should be stored in a dry place to help prevent mold contamination.

Concrete floors are not particularly good moisture barriers, so if the garage is the best home storage, for example, then lift the wood off the floor using inverted plastic buckets or drums that will be strong enough to hold the load. Hard wood could be used, but eventually any moisture from the floor will penetrate it too. Outdoor woodcarvings or wood sculptures should not be placed directly onto the ground for the same reasons. Metal moisture barriers may eventually rust unless thoroughly zinc galvanized or made from lead.

Spalting

Fungi exist in two forms, one that discolors without causing decay or loss of strength in the wood, and one that is destructive to the cells and causes rotting. Fungi exist in different colors, and these may stain or color the wood, sometimes creating dramatic and effective colored patterns, which is called *spalting*. The layers of staining are often referred to as *zone lines*.

Mold also represents a health hazard; it must not be inhaled or ingested, which may happen if it is contained in sawdust or if it has contaminated old furniture that is being restored.

Notes about Terms—Hardwood vs. Hard Wood

Hardwood is the common name for a botanical classification called *angiosperm*, which refers to the manner in which the seeds of the tree are produced. An angiosperm has seeds that are covered with a hard external layer. A hardwood is not necessarily hard (meaning of a high density that makes it difficult to work with hand tools like woodcarving chisels), and can in fact be quite soft, like balsa wood, which is a botanical hardwood.

For the woodcarver, a *hard wood* (two words) is clearly one that is difficult to work, and, needless to say, there is often much confusion with the definition.

WOOD BURL

A *burl* is a large, bulging knob that sometimes grows on the trunk or branch of a tree (**4-16**). It can be sawn off with a chain saw without interfering with the life of the tree. Inside the burl the wood grain is considerably swirly and interlocked, and there are numerous bud growths. The appearance is often very attractive, and for this reason burls are used in fancy wood turning.

Hand carving the burl presents some significant challenges. First, it is mostly impossible for the wood to support any kind of detail, since it will simply fracture. Second, a dry burl is often very hard and difficult to cut with hand tools (**4-17**). Certainly a heavy mallet is needed. Hand working is best done when the burl is wet. Holding burls still during carving is difficult because of their shape, and it may be necessary to chock it with wedges between the jaws in a vise.

4-16 This is a burl from the trunk of a tree. Sometimes burls are covered in bark and look like a large lump; sometimes they are dead and look like this. Inside the burl is some very fancy grain figure, as seen in 4-18.

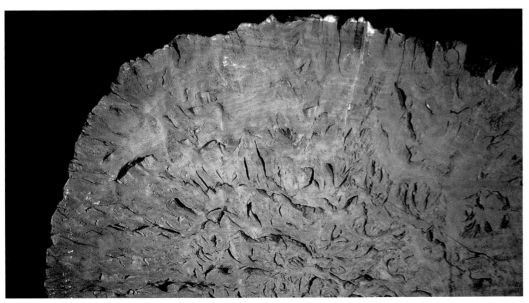

4-17 Burl when seasoned is normally tough and hard and very difficult to carve with hand tools. It can be turned on a wood lathe and is often used for fancy bowls.

4-18 *Here a knot has been used to advantage, forming "E.T.'s" eye. Be careful knots don't damage your tools since they can be hard and tough when the wood is seasoned.*

KNOTS

Knots can be a very attractive feature of wood or a frustrating nuisance for a carver. Of course, it all depends on the circumstances and the carver's intent; for relief carving in furniture a knot is most likely a definite problem, but for a found-wood sculpture it may be a decorative advantage.

A knot is a new branch that grows out of an existing trunk or branch. These new branches begin their life at the pith, which is the center and original part of the trunk or branch, and grow out through the wood more or less at right angles. They disturb the lay of the grain as they push their way through the existing wood, and there are typically swirling and wavy grain patterns surrounding them, which make working the wood difficult. Often the surrounding wood shrinks away from the knot as the wood dries after cutting, and the knots become loose and fall out.

Sometimes a knot develops as a very hard and dense part of the wood; it can damage tools to the extent that they are difficult to repair. As the grain in the knot is moving in the opposite direction to the grain in main piece, you may be cutting along the grain of a board or log and suddenly have to cut across the end grain of the new branch (**4-18**). We see an extraordinary example of nature at work in **4-19**!

Notes about Terms—Softwood vs. Soft Wood

The opposite of a hardwood is a *softwood* that is known in botanical terms as a *gymnosperm*. A gymnosperm, for example, a conifer, has seeds that are uncovered.

For the woodcarver, a *soft wood* (two words) is one that is mostly easier to work than a hard wood, although many softer woods can be spongy, stringy, and pulpy, making it difficult to achieve a good finish on them.

Harder woods often polish better than softer woods, because it is often easier to achieve a smooth surface. The woodcarver must experiment with different woods to develop a knowledge of those that perform best for the particular application. It is important not to assume that all softer woods are better for carving than all harder woods, and it is equally important not to become confused by the botanical definitions. If you are willing to try different species with a carving tool to "see what happens," you will very quickly achieve a working knowledge of many species that will make it easier for you to make future decisions.

4-19 In this amazing example, the perfect sculpture is created by nature herself—this piece of firewood was split open and there inside was another branch completely encased by the tree trunk

Chapter Five

DREAMING OF DRAWING?

Introduction to Drawing

Drawing is one of those artistic things that, like most of the others, falls into either the "I can do it" or the "I can't do it" category. If you have achieved some reasonable results so far with your carving and made some things you never thought you could, then now is the time to develop some good competence with drawing. Because you can do this too! The kind of drawing that will be most useful for woodcarving is relatively simple, so there is no need to fear you will have to become a second Picasso! Pencil drawing is best, as it is easiest to correct and needs the simplest of tools.

There are just four main ingredients needed to get started. The first two are the tools—you need the right kind of pencil, and the right kind of paper—and some other bits and pieces. Now this might seem a bit simple, because if you go to your art material supplier the range of both can be quite daunting. The second two are your observation skills and a relaxed state of mind.

FIRST—THE PAPER

Whether you buy a pad or book (spiral bound is very handy) or separate sheets, you will need a firm surface to rest it on. Stiff cardboard or a clipboard will be satisfactory in the absence of a firm backing on a pad or a book of paper.

The trade descriptions used for different kinds and grades of paper vary, including such names as cartridge paper, bank paper, Bristol board, bond, and so on. Some will be recycled, acid free, or bleached, or have some other description. Whatever they are, you can receive very good advice from your retailer as to what they all mean, while at the same time there are some fundamental things that make paper suitable or not for pencil drawing.

First, don't get paper that is too thin. It will tear or crumple easily and be a nuisance. Like timber, paper comes in grades, whether termed newsprint, Bristol, or bond, that are measured in terms of density. This is usually noted by the manufacturer in pounds (lbs) or grams per square meter (g/m²).

Bond paper that is very thin will be in the vicinity of 8 lbs (30 g/m²), and paper that is heavy will be generally over 80 lbs (300 g/m²). For reference, office photocopy paper is around the 20-lb (75-g/m²) mark, and is a bit thin for drawing and sketching.

A comfortable weight of paper for pencil sketching is about 36 lbs (135 g/m²).

As you look through the papers that are available, you will notice some are really very smooth and shiny, and others are coarse and spongy. The best for pencil drawing is neither, but more a matte finish and reasonably smooth. Once again for reference, the surface texture of standard office photocopy paper is quite acceptable. Most manufacturers will describe the suitability of their papers for drawing, and certainly your supplier can help you.

SECOND—WHICH PENCIL?

Pencils are numerous in their brands and varieties, as shown in **5-1**. However, once again, some basics will get you through:

Pencils come with "lead," which is really graphite compound, which varies in density from very hard to very, very soft. A distinguishing numbering standard may exist in your country, and this may have a hard pencil designated with a number such as 4H, a medium pencil designated HB, and a very soft pencil designated 6B.

Choose for your drawings four different kinds—2H, HB, 2B, and 6B. This will give you plenty of variety for most of the things you will want to do. The ones you will use most are HB and 2B. We will see for what later. Your retailer can advise which brand names will offer the best performance. Poor-quality pencils will constantly break; the wood they are made from will splinter and be difficult to cut away tidily when you want to sharpen them.

A substitute for a regular pencil is what is known as a clutch pencil, shown on the left in **5-1**.

5-1 On the left is a clutch pencil that can take different densities of lead refill. It is shown here with an HB lead and next to it left to right are regular pencils with 2H, HB, 2B, and 6B plus a solid graphite for shading, with samples of the kinds of lines they draw. Softer leads draw thicker, darker lines and are good also for shading; harder leads draw lighter, thinner lines and are good for detail. The HB pencil is a "good all-rounder."

THIRD—NOW FOR SOME OBSERVATION SKILLS

The human brain has extraordinary storage capacity and a great ability to manipulate things and interpret them. One thing our brains do very well is store image concepts, give them a name, and take no notice whatsoever of detail.

So when you say you know what a horse looks like, what you really mean (for most of us anyway) is that you remember the general concept of the shape of a horse. So if you see a horse, you will recognize it as being a horse. However, if you tried to actually draw your vision of a horse, chances are you could not do it. You have in your mind the concept of a horse, you can manipulate it to be a big horse, or a little one, and you can distinguish a baby one, and think of a horse in any color you like. But try to remember the detail of one, and draw it on paper, and you cannot.

Our mind has very cleverly stored an image concept and no detail. This is mostly because we took no notice of the detail in the first place, because it wasn't our objective to do so. All our objective was to do was to "look at a horse." To develop satisfactory drawing skills, what we need to do is alter our objective. It's that simple. We must alter our objective from "looking at a horse" to "observing the detail of the shape of a horse."

Let's choose an easy and readily available subject to demonstrate what is meant. No cheating now!

Just about every one of us uses a knife and fork at least once a day every day. Our knife and fork come from the same utility set that is used every day. Take your pencil and paper, and draw the fork you use every day. Can you actually do it? Compare your drawing to the actual fork, and you will realize just how little of any of the detail you actually absorbed. Yet if someone put in front of you six different-shaped forks to choose from, you would pick the shape you use every day.

Now while you have the fork in front of you, take a good look at it. Don't put pencil to paper, just observe. What is its length? The length of its handle. The length of the prongs. How many prongs are there in the head? How wide is it? Once you have observed and considered these things, draw a copy of your fork while it is in front of you.

And, just to see what happens, in a week's time, draw it again, from memory. Compare the three drawings, and you will see the difference between "looking" memory and "observant" memory.

Now, before we go any further, this does not mean we need to actually remember every little detail we see. Not at all. What we *do* need to remember is that there *was* detail—that there was something in particular that distinguished one fork from another, for example. Or a horse from a rhinoceros. We can always go back to our fork, and check a detail shape, or to our horse, and get the shape of its ear, or eye. So don't overload your system with trying to memorize tiny details. But *do* get your system to start to see that the horse's eye is a particular shape; it is different from a rhinoceros's eye. If you are in fact interested in horses, your mind will start to remember things about horses without your asking it to, and all because you asked it to observe the detail rather than just look at the whole.

Development of our observation skills of course takes time. For us to be happy about this, we need to be interested in the subjects we are observing. This "mindset" is a very important part of "art." So, to maximize the efficiency of developing our observation skill, pick some subject that interests you. Observe the things that you would ultimately want to carve in wood.

A keen gardener might pick leaves, flowers, and trees. Floral arrangements can make some very attractive wall panels. A keen watersports person might consider shells and fish. Whatever your interest, set out to take a greater interest in the actual detail on the object rather than just the broad recognition of overall shape and color.

This leads us to the last of our four ingredients, the state of mind we bring to our work. We will call this our "mindset disposition."

FOURTH—MINDSET DISPOSITION

The normal bustle of modern daily life can be quite stressful, without us realizing it. We may not ever notice tense muscles, jerky hand movements, or an inability to concentrate on detail for anything other than a few minutes. Do you have a hand tremor? Hold your hand out in front of you and see if it has a tremor.

If you do, it may have simple cause, like drinking a lot of coffee; if it cannot be explained, perhaps you should seek medical advice. Another likely source is stress, from tense muscles in your arm and hand causing the hand to be unsteady.

A stress condition that is as perceivable as this is not conducive to good drawing learning. Unfortunately, sometimes trying a new activity for the first time can be stressful too. This stress is commonly the result of worrying about what other people will think of what you have done, combined with trying to learn about it under time pressure. There are three things, then, that will help a great deal to establish the best mindset for having a reasonable go at drawing, particularly if we think we can't do it at all.

First we need to reduce as much as possible our ongoing state of stress, if we have one. Second, we must promise ourselves that we will not let anyone see what we are doing unless it is really our intention that they see our work, and, third, we must promise ourselves that we will not try to do our first drawings in a rush—we will allocate plenty of time.

If you find a comfortable, peaceful place to do the series of exercises discussed in this chapter, and you approach the whole subject in a relaxed, unconcerned, and unhurried way, then you will succeed.

FIRST STROKES

Just as we have done with our chisels and pieces of timber, we need to get used to how our drawing tools feel in our hands—the way our different pencils react to the paper and the pressure we apply to them. For this, we will do some basic scribbling, but in a controlled way, so that it starts to make sense in our minds.

Take up your 2B pencil—this is fairly soft, and we can make some easy impressions with light and dark strokes with it. Seat yourself in a comfortable position at a table or desk, or in a chair making sure you have a firm backing on the paper. A number of variations on some basic exercises you should try first with your soft pencils and then with your harder ones are shown in **5-2**. In each exercise, each stroke has two parts.

There is the downstroke and then, the upstroke. On the downstroke, place a firm pressure on the pencil; on the upstroke ease right off, and just touch the paper with the lead. Do some straight lines first. You will see that it is hard to actually make a straight line, simply because the mechanics of the hand don't want to. The hand wants to move in a curve. Don't fight this, as it will be too frustrating. All you need to do in the beginning is make dark strokes down and light strokes up, in a continuous series.

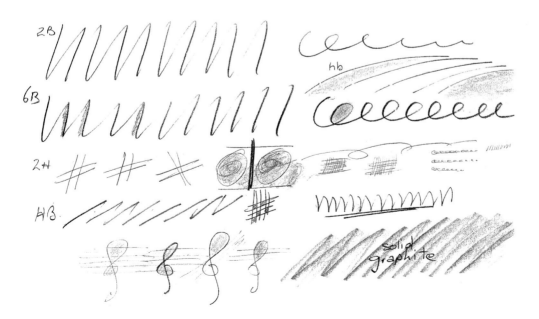

5-2 Practice upstrokes and downstrokes with different pencils and shade them in with the softer ones. Use exercises like these for loosening up before creating an actual drawing. Try different combinations of harder and softer pencils so that your familiarity with them becomes part of your skill bank.

When you have done some lines, do some circles. Make several pages of them, repeating over and over, and getting a feel for how the pencil behaves on the paper. As you make your lines and circles, be as free and easy as you can, without tension and hesitation in your hand. The strokes will become easier and easier to perform, and the darkness and lightness of the strokes on the paper will become more and more consistent. Your hand should feel quite loose and stress free. Each stroke should start to feel natural so that the transition from one to the other is smooth and willing. Each stroke should want the next stroke to happen.

Keep going page after page until it is so natural a movement that you start to create different shapes, densities, and sizes of stroke. As simple as these exercises seem, they are an easy and fun way to create a sensitivity between your hand and the pencil and paper so that when you come to some "real" drawing a little later, you will much more easily create the shapes you wish. You can use the exercises as a warmup each time you want to do some drawing.

The strokes you create are sometimes called *sweeps*. With your HB pencil create some curved sweeps, and with your 6B pencil shade them in. Practice light shading and heavy or dark shading. You will be using shading to represent shadows, which will also form part of our later discussions both about drawing, and also carving itself.

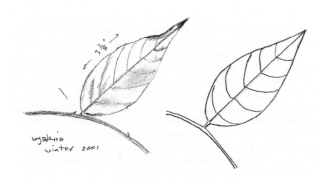

5-3 *Ensure symmetry actually exists before you draw it in a nature subject. The leaf on the right looks quite odd compared to the one on the left, which has no symmetry. The one with symmetry looks "juvenile," and obviously not drawn by someone who studied the leaf a little to observe its true characteristics.*

Now it is time to try a "real" drawing. We have chosen a simple leaf from the garden. Our example is a wisteria leaf (**5-3**). Choose something from your garden or a local park that has simple lines. Like most new activities, starting out with anything too complicated will only cause frustration, and most likely end up in your giving up. Choose something that is flat as well, so that there are no issues of depth and perspective to deal with.

Start with your HB pencil. Draw the outline of the leaf first. It doesn't really matter where you start. There are no rules, and you will most likely want to erase parts and redo them anyway. There are two parts of the outline that are particularly important. They are the shapes of the two ends. These are called *focal points* because they are parts of the leaf that are major determining factors of its overall appearance. The position of them will determine the length of the leaf, and the shape of them will determine key characteristics of the leaf.

The next most important thing is the width of the leaf at its widest part, and where this widest part is. This will clearly determine the overall size and shape of the body of the leaf.

Don't rush your drawing, don't feel embarrassed about using your eraser, and do draw the leaf several times. Each time you do, you will be surprised at the increasing speed and accuracy with which you do it.

Once you see that you have the outline of the drawings reasonably reproduced, place in the detail of the veins. Check the position of each vein carefully. Is there a center vein on your leaf? Are there small veins radiating from it? Do they actually join the center vein? Are they uniformly spaced? Are they parallel to one another? This part of the drawing really does need your focus on the observation of detail. This takes a little time to get used to, but once you do you will never look at a leaf the same way again!

The positioning of the veins and their thickness is quite important. If they are drawn uniformly distanced and meeting together in pairs at their ends, as shown on the right in **5-3**, they may well look artificial and unrealistic. If you are trying to reproduce an actual species, then accurate drawing is important. For nature subjects it is rare if ever that uniformity exists. There are no flat surfaces or straight and/or parallel lines.

Keep in mind, as discussed earlier, the left-hand side of a nature subject is rarely, if ever, the same as the right. To make them uniform may well make them look completely unnatural. It is unlikely that the right side of your head is the same exactly as the left side, or your right and left feet are exactly the same size, and so on.

Practice leaf drawing a few times. Keep all your attempts, so you can measure your progress. If you put in a few hours overall, you will be amazed at how you progress, and just how fast it is. Draw different kinds of leaf, each new one a little more complex than the last.

Once you start to see progress from your efforts, it's time to try drawing something quite different. Try a part of yourself! Place the index finger of your nondrawing hand over your sketch paper, and draw it with the other hand. First the outline, then the fingernail (a focal area), then the creases in the skin at the knuckles—these are focal lines (5-4). Try using different pencils for the skin creases. B or 2B may be too soft, and HB and/or 2H might be better. Don't press too heavily. Make light lines at the beginning, because they are easy to erase, and darker lines might be too heavy. They can always be gone over and made darker if necessary.

Once you have drawn your finger, try your big toe, or your whole foot. This will test your observation skills from a greater distance, and it will mean that because you can't shift your toe around as much as

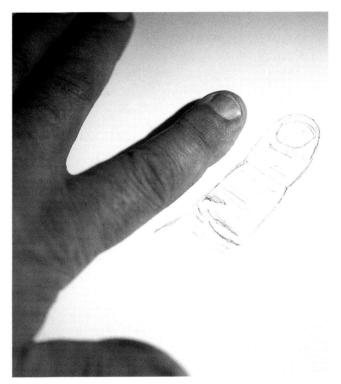

5-4 *Drawing part of yourself, such as your index finger or thumb, is a very convenient way to get some practice. You can look at it from all angles, place it wherever you like, and it won't disappear on you! Try out all your different pencils, and you will soon find the ones that best suit your own drawing style and the end results that you want.*

What about My Mistakes?

Use an eraser of course! For this there are excellent-quality synthetic "plastic" erasers, which will rub out errors without leaving behind a gray smeary mess.

Erasers are manufactured for different things, such as ink or pencil, and it is important to purchase one specifically for pencil. Choose a soft material rather than a hard one, so that it does not tear the surface of your paper as you rub it.

Graphite from your pencil will transfer to the eraser and leave a dirty surface, which you must remove so that you do not transfer that to the paper next time you use it. If it becomes dirty, simply rub it clean on some scrap paper.

As you use your eraser, waste material from it will collect on your paper, and this can soil the surface. Blow it away, or shake it off, rather than wiping it off with your hand, otherwise it might smudge the surface. Needless to say, store your eraser in a clean environment! A dirty eraser just transfers dirt!

your finger, you will have to get the lighting right so you can see all you need to see.

Try using a small reading light. You will probably find the best position for it is so that it casts a cross light over your foot or toe, and so that it is slightly elevated to enable you to get a good view of the top detail. If you have the light as vertically as you can over the foot so it doesn't interfere with your vision, you may not have as good a view of the skin wrinkles and toenail detail as you would like.

STYLIZED DRAWING

Abstract in the artistic sense means a form that has no basis in reality. We will look at it in Chapter 6, "Abstract Arrangements." *Stylized* means an impression of a real or imaginary object, which is generally recognized as being a likeness of a real thing, although it does not necessarily have any realistic detail. To draw in this manner and offer recognition of the real thing at the same time as creating something reasonably attractive is the test of the artist. Of course whether something is attractive, or not, is in the eye of the beholder.

An easy way to understand how stylized drawing might be developed is to place some tracing paper over a picture of a well-recognized object, such as an elephant, and try drawing different outlines, like the ones shown at the opening of this chapter on page 72. This kind of "kindergarten" drawing is a good way to come to terms with stylized drawing. The profiles are still recognizable as elephants, while at the same time they are fun to look at. Either one would make a great wooden desktop paperweight.

Try to develop a simple stylistic approach, and as you do, try to imagine how your sketches might look in wood. Think of them in dark wood, light wood, colored, and striped. Color some in with pencils to get a better understanding (5-5).

Modeling the two-dimensional sketches is the next step. Try front- and back-view drawings to go with your side-profile sketches (5-6). If you have no photographs to go on, these will test your imagination and memory bank. However, as we are dealing in impressions, provided the additional views are interesting and/or attractive, it will be fairly difficult to go wrong. There are no rules!

Should I Keep My Drawings?

This, of course, is entirely up to you; however, there are some very good reasons for storing them, at least for a reasonable time. First, if you haven 't really done any drawing before, it is a good idea to keep every-thing you do for a while because it becomes an amazing picture story of inspiration for you. If you do the exercises and try the ideas described below, over a very short time you will see an amazing improvement.

In a matter of hours you will be able to compare your starting point to where you are currently at; you will be amazed and inspired by what you see. This is a very important personal measure of your progress and success doing something you perhaps thought you could never do.

Second, if you form a habit of sketching or drawing things you see or think of, even if it is just shapes you are trying to visualize, over time you will build up quite a collection of reference material. These records may well come in handy many times over as a personal library of ideas. At the end of this chapter we will take a look at some hints for recording drawings so that they remain as a meaningful record of things you have seen, or ideas you have conceived.

For this reason, it is recommended that when you are purchasing your drawing paper, you give serious con-sideration to spiral-bound books of paper rather than pads of tear-out individual sheets. Buy one or two dif-ferent sizes of books of paper. Try 8½ × 11 for regular sketching and 6 × 9 inch for traveling.

5-5 Shade in some sketches to get the feel for how they might look in wood. Make a plasticine model or two as well. This will help you to develop the concept of converting your two-dimensional sketch to a three-dimensional in-the-round concept.

5-6 Use modeling to work out what the front, back, top, and bottom views might be. Once you have one or two you like the look of, commit them to paper alongside your original sketch. Use modeling in an interactive way to help sort out both your imagination and your drawing skills.

RECORDING INFORMATION IN THE FIELD

Finally, it is important, once you have decided to take the advice and keep records of things you think of and see, that you develop a simple discipline for actually keeping those records. This discipline will make the records meaningful and very usable at any time you return to them in the future.

What to Note

Here are some principles to follow, which are shown in a field book extract in **5-7**.

Note the date of the drawing. This helps keep things in order, and, if it is a nature subject of a seed or a flower, for example, the drawing date will give you a seasonal reference if you need to find another sample in a few years' time.

Note the place where the drawing or sketch was done. If you need to go back there, you needn't rely on a failing memory to guide you.

Record some accurate measurements—at least height, width, and thickness. Guessing proportions months after an event can produce some very unsatisfying and misleading results.

Drawing the cross sections at key points of the object is very useful for the determination of proportion at a later date. You can record thickness of parts of the cross section, and this is very useful as well.

Record characteristics of any shadowing accurately. When you do, it may not look wonderfully artistic, but at least it will be an accurate reflection of the shape. If you record shading to make the drawing look pretty rather than realistic, you may well make the carving of it difficult later on. Don't try to be a "wonderful" artist, but rather an *accurate* one.

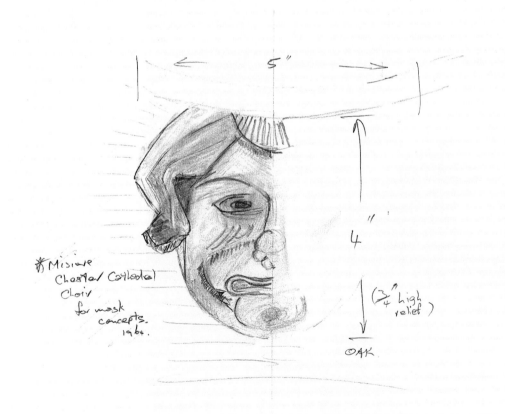

5-7 *This page comes from a field sketchbook recording details of a carving in a cathedral. Note that the scale of the drawing and the location of the carving in the church are recorded. You might want to go back years later to find it again. Sometimes the furniture may be moved or stored; if the name or description of the item of furniture is recorded, then it possibly can be found in its new home.*

Other Handy Instruments & Drawing Techniques

You might find it useful to have a rule for measuring, a T-square for drawing right angles (you might want to draw a frame around a sketch), a clip or two for holding paper down. If you need to hold paper still for tracing, for example, use some nonpermanent adhesive tape rather than pins. Pins tend to allow the paper to tear, and as a result it will always move at the wrong time.

And you might want some plasticine or similar material for holding leaves or flowers still (use it for packing underneath to hold them up on a tabletop, for example).

One of the most useful drawing techniques is the grid method, as shown in **5-8**, for enlarging or reducing patterns. The grid method can also be used for transferring a design to the wood. If you want to use the grid method you will need a rule.

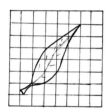
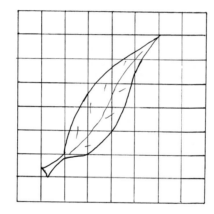

5-8 *For enlarging or reducing your drawings you can use the grid method as illustrated. Divide each area into the same number of grid squares and transfer your pattern.*

If you do purchase plastic drawing instruments such as a rule, make sure you get clear see-through ones so you can see your drawing. It makes them much easier to use.

ABSTRACT ARRANGEMENTS
Having Some Fun with Abstract Sculpture

Here we take a look at some fun things you can have a go at without having to spend a lot of time or money tracking down raw materials. We will ask what exactly do we mean when we say something is abstact. We explore a way to get going by taking a recognizable shape and stylizing it. In this straightforward process we can free up our thinking to generalize shapes and create something that gets us on the way to thinking abstractly.

WHAT IS ABSTRACT?

What is *abstract?* What does it mean? In art, an abstract is a form or shape that is often geometric and does not represent a particular thing. In writing, an abstract is a summary of what is written. So if you were to summarize part of this book into its essential elements, you would be producing an abstract from it; if you look at **6-1**, you will see an abstract drawing.

Depending on its context, then, abstract can have different meanings. For some of us, every time we doodle on paper we are creating abstract forms. We create meaningless (but not necessarily unattractive) shapes of all kinds. For the rest of us, particularly if we have very organized minds, an abstract shape is something that we tend to create only with a fair amount of effort.

Now, if you are one of these people, or somewhere in between being a highly organized thinker and a regular abstract doodler, then one way to start to get the hang of it all is to take a regular shape and remove the detail. Create something from it that isn't strictly abstract, but rather a stylized representation that is still recognizable. What you will be doing is freeing up your thinking process from the constrictions of organization and applying some creative juices to make generalized shapes. You are on the way to abstract thinking.

HOW CAN I DO SUCH A THING?

Try this: Find a photograph of a familiar object. and have a go at drawing a freehand childish sketch that is a bit stylized. Take a look again at page 74. There, at the opening of Chapter 5, "Dreaming of Drawing?" we chose an elephant. If you already drew the elephant for that chapter then raid your child's animal books and see what you can find to have a go at something dif-

ferent. The important thing is to start yourself on the path to free thinking! Take a recognizable shape, remove details, and make it stylish and fun. Just like you did in kindergarten! Do several for yourself, and you will be amazed at how quickly you start to lose the systematic approach and revert to your more natural freedom of thought. If you do use the elephant, make

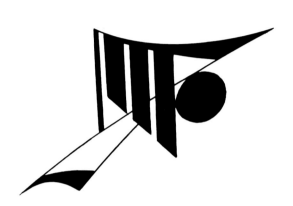

the four legs into two, don't draw in the ear itself but just make a curved line representing it; as for the trunk, well—experiment!

Thinking in terms of the abstract is not easy. Certainly we often see someone else's abstract work and say "I don't understand that!" or we ask, "What's that supposed to be?" Having a go ourselves is not something we would consciously do. However, if you would like to free up your thinking, its something you have to try! Once you have drawn your stylized elephant, or your dog or cat or partner,

6-1 This is an abstract drawing. It represents nothing in particular at all, but it does create a form that has dimensions that can be interpreted however you like.

move on and create a blob or two. Get disorganized and you'll have a lot of fun on paper! All you have to do is transfer that fun to your piece of wood. So let's select some wood to work with.

CHOOSING SUITABLE WOOD

Each of the abstract arrangements presented here has been made from some western red cedar bought from the local lumberyard. If you buy a piece from a board dressed down from its rough-sawn measurement of 8 inches by 2 inches and 3 feet long you will have enough for the three abstracts.

Western red cedar is not a usual carving wood, because it is too soft and pulpy, and splits easily so that it cannot sustain any detail. However, for these abstracts, there is no detail, so with care you will be able to achieve some fun pieces to decorate your desk. It is also an easily procurable commercial timber.

Storing Wood—Things to Do

Raise wood off concrete floors with a water-proof barrier such as plastic sheeting or blocks to prevent mold growth.

Separate boards in a stack with thin strips of wood (stickers) to allow all-round ventilation. Ensure the stickers are of equal thickness so the boards will not bend. Ventilation allows the wood to maintain an even moisture content to avoid warping.

Store out of direct sunlight and wind to prevent fading, heat, and fast-drying, which can cause the cells to dry out and shrink and the wood to crack.

Seal the ends (the end grain) of boards, logs, and blocks with an effective water barrier, so that moisture loss is from the sides—the long grain. This helps prevent cracking. Old paint, particularly acrylic, is mostly unsatisfactory as a barrier. Beeswax or candle wax, or a brush on commercially available timber end sealer, is best.

Leave bark on logs intact to help slow down moisture loss. The slower the drying process, generally the less the cracking.

Store boards flat (horizontally), not on their ends, unless it can be ensured they will not bend.

Store small logs on their ends, and rotate frequently end to end to ensure equal moisture dispersal along their length. If they are stored on their sides, ensure all-round ventilation, and roll them frequently.

Lift the ends of small logs off the floor with a small block of wood to ensure good ventilation. Too much moisture from within the log collecting around the end of it may cause mold growth. Treat blocks in the same manner as logs.

Storing Wood—Things NOT to Do

Do not store wood in the trunk of your car, near radiators or other heaters that cause moisture reduction, especially wood fires.

Do not store wood in direct sunlight or wind that could result in fading, heat, and fast-drying, which can cause the cells to dry out and shrink and the wood to crack.

Do not store wood in a dehumidified air-conditioned environment unless it is gradually conditioned to it.

Do not move wood from one set of humidity conditions to another (for example across state to a different climate) without taking suitable precautions. A dryer climate may cause cracking, and a wetter climate may cause buckling. Sometimes it is best not to move acclimatized objects at all, particularly if they are made from multiple parts, such as a rocking horse.

Avoid importing wooden items from a country with a significantly different climate. For example, importing from an Asian country with a humidity level of 85 percent to a climate with 30 percent is a recipe for damage.

Do not completely cover unseasoned wood with a moisture barrier unless it is to be kept wet. Leave the side or long grain uncovered for moisture to escape, so that seasoning can occur.

Do not put wood you have collected from the garden or the outdoors with your other wood until you have cleaned it thoroughly as we discussed in Chapter 4, "Natural Wonders." When you find that you have a need to prepare for carving some found wood of this sort, especially be alert to fungus and insects that cause decay. A few simple precautions will ensure your successful use of the wood.

Before we get started, we should look at the sidebars, on the opposite page and this one, about what to consider when we store wood at home and how we can prepare it for carving. Being an organic substance, wood is prone to damage if it is not looked after properly. Nothing we discuss about caring for your wood is difficult to do, but if these things aren't done, the the wood could become difficult or impossible to use.

PLANNING THE FINISHING BEFORE WE GET STARTED

As a part of the planning process, we should consider what we want the final carving to look like. Do we want it looking natural? Glossy? Are we going to paint it? Wax it? There are many options with modern synthetic finishes; however, one option that is often overlooked is oiling.

In medieval times oil was about the only commonly available finish, and walnut oil was often the one. For our "Abstract Arrangements," we will try one of the many readily available oils from our local deli or supermarket, such as cooking oil or salad oil. Two others you could track down and try are orange oil (which may add a golden hue to the wood) and tung oil (from the Chinese tung tree, which produces a soft sheen and will make the wood darker). These two oils may be available only at a specialized woodwork tool supplier.

Natural oils make excellent finishes for carved wood. Vegetable oils are good finishes for kitchen utensils, but will need replenishing after using and washing. With some softer and more open-grained woods, natural food oils may raise the grain and make the surface "woolly" in appearance; the oil may make the surface softer and less resistant to damage. Oils generally will make the surface darker; if the surface is subsequently damaged, the oil may be squeezed away, and that part of it may appear lighter than the rest. Try olive oil, sunflower oil, and peanut oil.

Nut oils are a good choice where high shine is not required. In addition to walnut oil try macadamia and almond oil (which is colorless). After many repeated applications of natural oils, it is possible to achieve a low to medium sheen, particularly with fine-grained timbers which do not allow extensive absorption. Let the oils dry and set hard between applications.

Preparing Wood for Carving— Things to Do

Check whether the wood is seasoned or wet before commencing carving, and treat it accordingly during the carving process. Unseasoned wood has a higher water content than dry wood; this can often be detected by a wet feel, a wet smell, or a darker color (wet wood is often darker than dry).

Trim the wood to the required finished dimensions before commencing carving, unless some extra wood is needed for clamping in a holding device. Cutting after the event may cause damage to the work, and because the wood is no longer a regular shape it may be impossible to hold safely for cutting.

If the carving is an integral part of other woodwork such as cabinetmaking or wood turning, plan for the carving by leaving sufficient extra material on the component so that there is something to take the carving.

It is best to plane off surfaces to be carved rather than leave them rough sawn as it is easier to see the grain and to apply drawing.

Preparing Wood for Carving— Things NOT to Do

Do not sand the surface before carving, as any residual sanding grit will cause damage to your finely sharpened tools. If you do sand, vacuum the surface to clear any grit.

Do not use screws to hold the wood to a baseboard for carving without first checking that the screws will not interfere with the carving tools as the carving progresses.

GETTING STARTED ON AN ABSTRACT CARVING

Let's get the ball rolling by making a stylized saxophone (**6-2**). Or at least maybe that's what it is! No new tools are needed for this project.

Once you have cut the profile as shown in **6-3**, it is time to give some serious thought to just how you would like your stylized sax to look. Follow the sug-gested ideas if you want, but if you have some of your own that you prefer, then use them! You will find it easy to decide what you want if you work it out on paper first. You might change your mind as you carve, but at least this will get you started.

The carving of these abstract arrangements is very easy. The only thing that may be a little difficult is hold-ing them during carving. The easiest way is to use your bench hook, as well as a jaw-type vise. The wood we chose is extremely soft, so once the forming of the shape is done with the gouge and skew, the smoothing is easily and quickly done with sandpa-per. You can supplement this with sanding drums on your power drill for extra fast performance.

With all these sorts of abstract shape, the nature of, and relationship among, the curves is the most important part. Avoid curves with kinks, uneven sweeps, and straight sections in them. Whatever

6-2 *This is a stylized drawing of what might have been a saxophone. Use this illustration, or draw your own from something that you like. If you enlarge this on a photocopier, make it about 10 inches high. We have begun the planning of our actual carving. Making these kinds of notes is a good way to get started; if you are one of those who is organized and finds it hard to be a "free thinker," then this little bit of discipline will make you feel at home!*

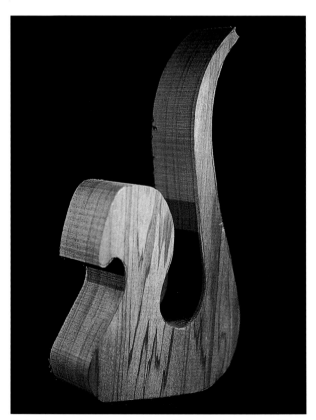

6-3 *Here is the saxophone profiled on a band saw. You could also use a scroll saw for this very soft wood, or cut by hand with a coping saw.*

6-4 When you use your bench hook, if you firmly rest your wrist on the sax and push in toward the back cleat of the bench hook, the wood will be easily held in place. Resting your wrist and holding the tool low down on the blade also increases the control you have over the tool and makes carving easier and more accurate.

your selection of curves, make them interesting, flowing, and blending with one another. Follow a geometric approach at first, and you will soon see how the relationships of flowing curves and a sprinkling of angles can make for attractive and fun decorative objects.

With your saxophone, once you have an idea of what you want, make sure your gouge and skew are very sharp; start with the bowl end by chamfering off the corner and removing some of the waste on the reverse side. The body of the instrument can be thinned down as well, and all this can be done using your bench hook as support.

Sometimes these awkward shapes can invite unsafe carving technique; there is a great temptation to hold the wood in one hand and gouge in the other. This is a very unsafe practice and must be avoided. Rest your carving on the back of the bench hook and hold it still with your wrist (**6-4**). Complete your carving to your desired shape, sand it smooth (**6-5** and **6-6**).

Sand the abstract to a fine finish before oiling, as shown in the opening photo for this chapter on page 84. Make sure you have removed any blemishes. With softer woods like Western red cedar, sanding is a fast process and can cause a lot of damage. Do not use a coarse paper, but rather a fine one no less that 180 grit. This is done with 220 then 600 grit for a final smoothness. Oil your creation with some cooking oil from the kitchen, or some gourmet oil from the deli. It is always wise to

test any finish on an offcut to make sure you like the effect. Once you have applied a finish such as oil, it cannot be removed, so test it first. Add some keys if you are inspired. Now, put on your favorite jazz CD!

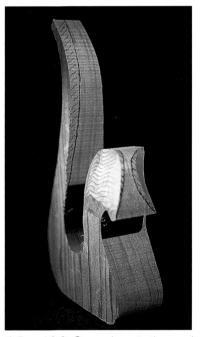
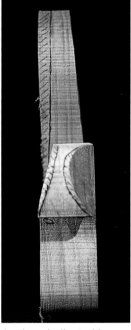

6-5 and 6-6 Carve down to the required depth as indicated by your guidelines. If you change your mind, that's okay! In this example, we have decided to leave the sax fairly chunky and square—as opposed to the roundness they have in real life—and leave the curves to the profile itself plus some suggestions of curve on the bowl and the U of the body.

SOME MORE POSSIBILITIES

If you would like to try your hand at some more stylized carvings, check out these two pages for some simple but attractive fun. Try these designs—or use them to inspire you to make up your own. They are both abstracts, but no doubt you can make something out of them if you let your imagination run free. They are made by following exactly the same process as for your saxophone, the same tools, and finished with oil.

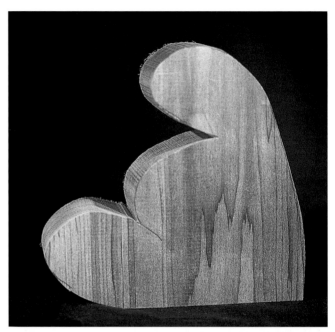

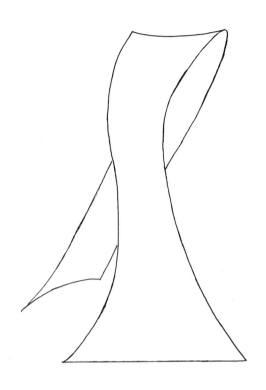

Chapter Seven

ROUNDER RUMBLINGS
Carving in the Round

When you have completed each of the carvings in the previous chapters, you will have progressed from fundamental whittling, experimented with some relief carving, explored the beauty of found wood sculpture, and played with some drawing and abstract arrangements. Now, it is time to combine them all as we work from the single view of a color photograph from the local zoo. For our next creative exploit we have chosen a pigmy hippopotamus. The snapshot we will use to develop our design is typical of the photographs you will take, not knowing that one day you will want to carve the subject. As a consequence, you only have one view, and you suddenly wish you had taken a lot more!

CREATING A PATTERN

What we need to do in this project is use our imagination to visualize the other views that we don't have, with our source photograph, **7-1**, as our starting reference. Start with a pattern for the side view, by simply taking our snapshot of the pigmy hippopotamus and doing a fairly representational tracing (**7-2**). Now, unless we are experts on the pigmy hippo, all we can do is make up the rest as we go along. Provided we do not try to pass our model hippo off as having been done from a real one and provided that the carving is generally plausible in its shape, we can have a lot of fun creating an attractive piece that will be more than acceptable to other nonpigmy-hippo experts!

CHOOSING OUR WOOD

For this little hippo, we have chosen common European elm from a local garden. You will need a small block for this carving; here we will be starting with a piece 8 inches long, 3 inches thick, and 3 inches wide.

7-1 This is a snapshot picture of a pigmy hippopotamus at the local zoo. As we do not have any other views of our subject, we will have to use our imagination to fill in the blanks.

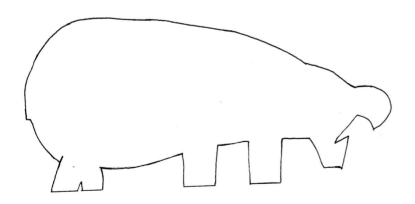

7-2 You can use this drawing, which is basically a simple tracing of the photograph. You will need to copy onto your wood using the grid method, freehand, or photocopying to the required size to suit your wood.

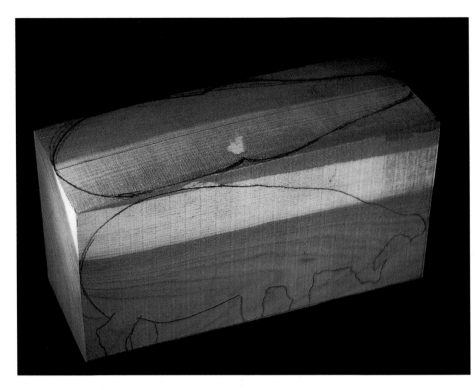

7-3 Starting with a block that is about eight inches long and three inches square, we have transferred the side view pattern to the wood, and then invented a top view. We have chosen to retain some of the sapwood for our carving, for creative effect.

Choosing Wood for Carving in the Round

When we are choosing wood for carving in the round, there are a few points that we should consider (see also Chapter 2, "Kidding Around").

If the project is a large sculptural piece, where fine detail is not a requirement, it is possible to achieve good results with grainy, coarser timbers. In these cases, the softer woods such as western red cedar and Radiata pine that you might reject for carving in relief for fine furniture might just be very appropriate.

Most woods will allow you to carve across the grain with reasonable ease and little breaking up of the wood. Being able to carve across the grain is very useful for carving in the round, because of the constant changing of tool direction needed to create the round shapes. Some woods, however, are not particularly good for across-grain carving. These include black willow, tropical kauri, and Douglas fir. If you have any doubt, test the wood first with a sharp gouge.

You will need to hold the wood still by either screwing it to a board at its base, and clamping that to a bench-top, or by placing it in a vise. If the latter is to be used, ensure the wood will not easily bruise as it might get quite damaged during the carving process. Woods that are too soft and have very low impact resistance are unsuitable. If you use a screw method, a really soft wood may allow the screws to come loose under constant pressure.

The larger the carving and the denser the wood, the heavier it will be. Be careful not to embark on a project that you literally can't handle!

The hippo we will cut using a band saw from a piece of branch that includes some yellow-colored sapwood. The heartwood of elm is a mid-brown color. Elm allows you to cut across it with ease and no tearing, and it is firm enough to resist damage from the jaws of a vise provided care is taken. Our hippo has reasonably thick legs, so although the grain will run across them (that is, along the length of the body), together with the natural strength of the elm wood, the legs will not easily break. No new tools are needed for this project; access to a band saw is useful, but a coping saw will work just as well.

If you find that you cannot easily obtain some elm, you could choose from many other species, including American black walnut, Mexican cocobolo, or Andaman padauk.

TRANSFERRING THE PATTERN

We start by transferring to the wood the side view pattern that we have traced from the photograph (7-3). We have also invented the top view and drawn it in place on the wood. It is reasonable to deduce from the photograph that the hippo is narrower at the front end than the rear and that he has a relatively small head. The proportions are plausible and look right even if they are not precise.

CUTTING PROFILES

We have cut the side profile first, saving the offcut to use as a guide to cut the top profile (7-4). You may do the top profile first if you wish. Either way save the off-

7-4 *The side profile was cut first using a band saw. Either profile can be cut first as long as the offcut piece with the uncut profile is retained. The offcut piece that has the other profile pattern will be put back in its original position as a guide for cutting.*

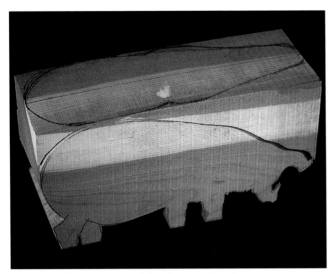

7-5 *The offcut is put back in place so that the top pattern drawn on it can be used as the next cutting guide.*

cut to use as a guide for cutting the next profile, as we are doing in **7-5**. If you don't think you can hold the offcut still on the band saw, for safety's sake you can use some double-sided tape to stabilize it. This is, however, mostly unnecessary. Now that both profiles are cut, the sharp corners and flat edges need to be smoothed (**7-6**).

MARKING THE FEATURES FOR CARVING

As you begin removing the sharp edges, you need to stop and think about how to carve the legs and feet. Turn the hippo on its side and study the ridges, giving thought to how the legs should be aligned, as discussed in **7-7**. You will find it helpful to use different colored crayons to indicate what should be preserved and what is waste to be cut (**7-8, 7-9, 7-10**).

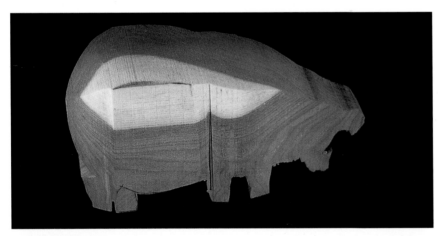

7-6 *This is the hippo with both profiles cut. The first principle of carving in the round for a nature subject is that there should be no sharp corners and no flat edges—they simply don't exist—so wherever there is one it must be removed.*

7-7 *If you turn your hippo on its side, you will see the ridges, marked with the colored dots, somewhere along which are the four feet, and the lower teeth in the case of the red dot. The pair of rear feet and the pair of front feet are not in the same line from side to side as the hippo is walking. The thighs must be carved in the same line as one another (although it does not look like this in the drawing or this rough-cut block), so these ridges are positioning guides for the feet (and teeth) only.*

7-8 *Using different-colored crayons, mark on the position of the feet (shown in white); this will in turn indicate the waste to be removed (shown in red). The teeth can also be marked although this can wait until later.*

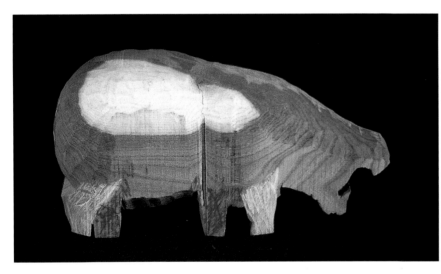

7-9 *Stand the hippo back up on its "feet," and you can mark in the side parts of the block that need to be removed (shown in red). In this illustration you can see the rounding-off process is well and truly underway. Start by removing the sharp edges of the corners with the gouge and working your way across the flat surfaces until they are round. Use a reasonably flat (but not completely flat) gouge and the "scallops" will not be too severe. You can see the scallops clearly around the tummy area in this illustration.*

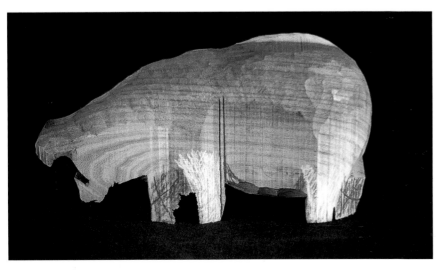

7-10 *It is important to do both sides and to remember that one foot will be in front and one behind the other as he walks. For our four-legged friends there are typically two legs on the same side pointing together and two on the opposite side pointing apart. If you do not work consistently around your carving in the round, you run a great risk of making it lopsided; depending on how far you have gone, it may not be repairable. For larger carvings in the round, you can draw centerlines for easy measuring reference.*

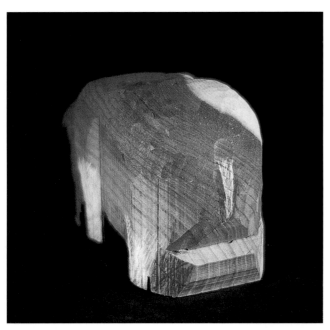

7-11 *Not to be forgotten is our hippo's tail—here we are using white for the tail and again red for the wood to be removed around it to expose it. When cutting "end grain," you may need your mallet because carving may be more difficult depending on how dense your piece of wood is.*

When you are cutting along the sides of the hippo, you are cutting long-grained wood, and it will carve easily. When you are cutting around the rear end of the hippo, you are cutting more "end grain," and the carving may be more difficult depending on how dense your piece of wood is (7-11). The denser it is, the harder it is to cut the end grain. You may need your mallet for this area if you are not already using it.

Removing Waste

Start removing the waste from around the leg areas while being careful not to cut off the leg you want to keep (7-12). Take care when holding the piece in your vise (7-13). Don't panic if there is an accidental breakage; simply glue it back on with a good wood glue. If you carefully glue it on immediately after it breaks off, no glue line should be visible in the finished carving.

SHAPING

Once the legs are largely free of waste, continue shaping the carving (7-14). Elm generally cuts very cleanly; since it is not too dense, your gouges will remain sharp

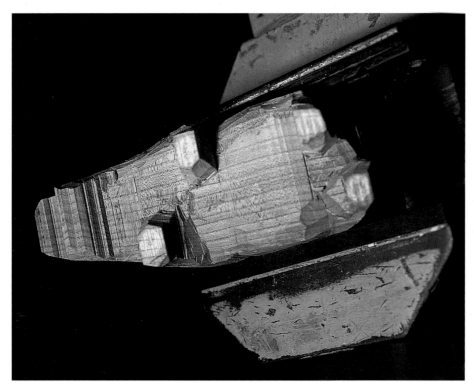

7-12 *Here we see the waste removed from around the leg area (marked earlier in red). If you are using a vise with metal jaws, it is imperative that you do not hit your sharp gouge into them. Severe damage will result. Help protect them by lining the jaws with wood, or as in this case with thick rubber material.*

7-13 Here we see the hippo being held in the same vice jaws as *7-12*, but this time by the feet. This is a much more stable position than in the previous illustration because in that one the roundness tends to make it harder to hold it stable. Unfortunately, putting pressure on the feet in this manner may also lead to broken legs unless they are thick enough and exactly the same length so there is no uneven pressure. If the wood is cut accurately, there is no reason why the legs will be uneven; if reasonable care is taken, breaks can usually be avoided, at least in the early stages of the carving process.

7-14 Here we see the rounding process continuing all over the animal, with just a small flat area left on the side. The left rear thigh is in the making, the nose is being rounded, and the bottom jaw is being thinned and is ready for a decision about the large teeth.

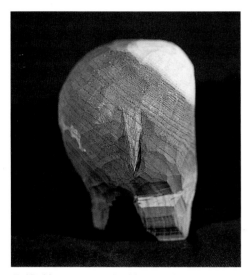

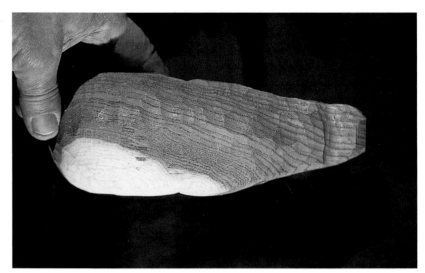

7-15 Here we see the hippo right way up from the rear end, showing what it looks like with one side round and the other square. If your hippo looks like this from any view, it is urgent that you even things up before progressing any further.

7-16 This is the top view of our uneven beast. Notice how it looks like it is bending off to the left? This is because the right side of the head has been cut away and not the left. Before going any further, correct this too. Now, of course at different points in time the sides must be uneven until you get to work on them both. But what we are saying is that you must be aware of this and constantly check that you are not creating an imbalance that is too hard to fix.

for a good time. If they start to get blunt, you will notice each cut getting rougher and rougher and the gouge harder to push through the wood. Use your strop frequently, for best results.

As you round the carving pay attention to the overall look of the figure (**7-15, 7-16**). When the rounding is uneven, if you continue to round off the side that is already round, chances are you will make it smaller, you will go too far, and your proportions will be wrong. To correct such an error, you will have to make the whole animal smaller. It is very important to work consistently around the whole animal, to avoid a lopsided carving (**7-17, 7-18**). Carving in the round is exactly that—carving it all the way round all of the time!

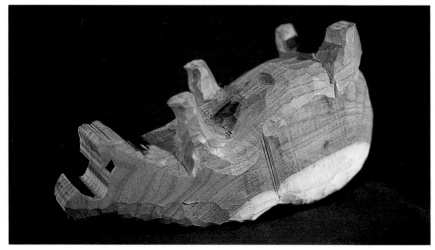

7-17 Seen upside down, you can clearly see that there is a greater area of flat surface on this side of the hippo. Three of the legs have been thinned down with the left rear untouched. It is very important, as was explained earlier, that you work consistently around the whole of the animal, to avoid your carving's becoming lopsided. Before progressing any further with other parts of the carving, cut this side to the same degree of roundness as the other side.

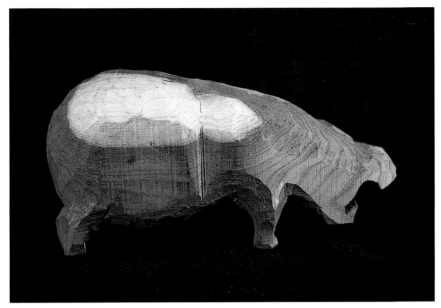

7-18 *This is the upright view of **7-17**. There is a lot of flat area still to be removed. As previously mentioned, make a flat area round by working it from the corners first. If you work it from the flat first, you run the risk of simply digging a hole in the side, or at best keeping it flat but making it thinner overall. In the case of our hippo, start with the corners, along both top edges, and make the top itself round; then work this down the sides to the tummy.*

Finishing Ideas—Shoe Polish

Shoe polish is a good source of stain for altering wood color. The pigment is carried by the wax and impregnates the wood grain. The polish may be added layer after layer (adding more pigment to the wood each time) until a soft sheen is achieved. If the wood surface is not sealed first, the polish and its pigment will penetrate the wood unevenly, according to the configuration of the cells and fibers; those cells that are cut on the surface by a chisel will absorb polish that whole cells won't absorb. Patchy or blotchy staining may result.

The same applies, of course, to any stain. Shoe polish does not provide to the wood a large volume of pigment at one time, so color change will also be very gradual. Once applied to an unsealed surface, shoe polish is also impossible to remove. Given these shortcomings, it is wise to test the polish on an offcut of the wood before applying it to the finished work.

Finishing Ideas—Varnishes

There is a wide range of modern surface finishes that are generically referred to as varnish. These might be more correctly called polyurethane or epoxy resin finishes. Varnish in its original sense was usually a mix of a solvent such as alcohol or natural oils mixed with different natural resins. These kinds of varnish form hard surface coatings and have good durability qualities. If you intend to apply a varnish directly to an otherwise untreated (unsealed) surface, it is a good idea to first test the varnish on an offcut to ensure compatibility.

Woods with high resin content, such as some pines, may react unfavorably to oils or solvents; very porous woods may allow great penetration with little residual surface coating. For a surface that is highly carved, the gloss normally associated with varnish may be an inappropriate "look," and uneven penetration will most likely be unattractive.

DETAILING & FINISHING

Once you are happy with the overall shaping of the animal, work on the details of the head, teeth, and final shaping of the legs and feet (**7-19, 7-20**). Make your carving as detailed as you like, but remember that the more detail you add, the more correct it will have to be, otherwise it will start to look quite "wrong." The simplicity of the carving lends itself to being stylized more than accurate, so making it less stylized will place demands on accuracy that we don't have, because we haven't got the correct information in the first place!

As you progress with the rounding of your little hippo, you will be wondering about what to put on it as a surface finish. It is always best to seal the surface of your carvings, since house dust is very invasive and difficult if not impossible to remove from the pores of wood. For our hippo, we chose to seal it with a readily available clear liquid wood sealer from the local hardware store. Sometimes they are referred to as sanding sealers.

First sand the hippo as smooth as you want it, using paper of around 120-grit size (it is stamped on the back of the sheet). Then apply the sealer. An excellent easy finish to apply is furniture wax; just two or three applications will achieve a low sheen, as in the photo on the opening page of this chapter, page 92, as well as in **7-19, 7-20**, and **7-21**.

Finishing Ideas—Brush-on Stains

The changing of a wood's natural color is a subject of great debate and often many, sometimes confusing alternative solutions. The debate is mostly about the aesthetics of color alteration and the artistic merit of doing it. As the artistic value in the end remains the prerogative of the carver, it will not be discussed here. It is important, however, to note some of the difficulties that may be encountered in the general process of wood staining:

Depending on the nature of the cellular structure of the wood and the impact carving has had on the integrity of the cell vessels, wood stain will be "taken up" or absorbed by the wood in an irregular manner, which may cause a blotchy appearance.

Wood stain that has penetrated the structure of the wood cannot be easily removed, if at all.

If a further finish is to be applied over the stain, its chemistry must be compatible with the chemistry of the stain. Follow the manufacturer's instructions or seek advice.

A wood sealer applied to the surface before the stain is applied may help to ensure an even color, but once again its chemistry must be compatible to that of the stain.

While every care is taken by a manufacturer to ensure accurate color descriptions and color charts, the carver must nevertheless be prepared for results that may not meet expectations.

It is vital to test the proposed stain on a sample of the wood before it is applied to the finished carving. Experimenting with sealers underneath, and surface polishes over, the stain is essential to minimize the risk of permanent damage to the carving.

7-19 *Next carve in his two large bottom teeth. Here we have added some smaller ones at the top by simply cutting some shallow grooves along the top jaw with a V tool. The carving is fairly stylized; we can be detailed only to the extent that we have full and accurate information.*

7-20 *The legs of a real pygmy hippo are much thinner than ours, but leaving them thick and plain as we have doesn't detract from the fun nature of the carving. Notice that we have managed to achieve a fairly even rounding from the earlier problem we had with the flat sides.*

7-21 *Our stylized hippo—all derived from only one view in our starting photograph. Amazing what you can get away with if you don't try too hard, and what you can't get away with if you do!*

Chapter Eight

CHIPPING AWAY
Creating Incised Patterns with Chip Carving

Making repetitive borders for boxes and picture frames, or geometric patterns for drink coasters, or combinations of patterns and lettering for signs are just some of the popular things you can do with chip carving. Chip carving is the art of creating fine incised patterns. Traditionally, chip carving has used geometric shapes; however, the term now refers to any incised pattern. The carver needs to experiment with different patterns and practice various cuts to develop a facility with chip carving; but even with the first cut, you will be learning valuable things.

APPLICATIONS OF INCISED CARVING

For the woodcarver, incised means *cut in*. Letter carving is a good example of incised work. Incised lettering makes excellent signs, as shown in the two examples in **8-1** and **8-2**,

The application of a repetitive incised border pattern is delightfully displayed with this potato and pumpkin bin shown on the opposite page. This example shows how mainstream home carpentry and cabinet-making can be enhanced with thoughtful chip-carving decoration. Use repetitive chip-carving patterns to decorate a wide range of objects, even crucifixes (**8-3**).

SUITABLE WOOD FOR INCISED WORK

Key to the successful appearance of incised work is accuracy around the borders or edges of the incisions and consistency in the depth of the cuts. Generally, this means that the wood needs to be easy to cut so that great control can be maintained during each cut. This is why harder woods are not particularly appropriate.

Chip carving works best with soft timber, making the cutting process easier than it would be in harder wood, and featureless wood, so there is no interference to the pattern from figure and color variation in the wood. Woods to try are basswood (linden), jelutong, white beech, yellow pine, and poplar.

This does not mean that harder woods should be automatically excluded; however, they will probably best be tackled after considerable practice has developed the necessary

skills of tool control. Stringy and grainy woods, whether they are hard or soft, are also mostly inappropriate for incised work, as they can be difficult to clean up at the bottom or junction of the cuts, particularly when the junctions fall along the grain. Before embarking on an incised project it is best to test the proposed wood to ensure its suitability. Sapwood is also often more stringy than heartwood, making clean incised work difficult to achieve.

8-1 Incised carving is especially suitable for lettering. The selection of fonts can be made very easy by using any one of the hundreds that are available with most personal computers. Spacing the lettering is an important part of the overall look and should be done with care.

8-3 The use of repetitive geometric incised patterns is common and popular for symbolic decoration. Celtic-style designs offer substantial and attractive choices. The traditional chip pattern on this crucifix is not difficult but requires patience to execute. Care must especially be taken when the drawing is executed, making sure that the divisions, which form each chip, are the same size and shape. Very attractive designs can be achieved with practiced skill.

8-2 A wide range of fonts can be used for signage. The choice can be matched to the message of the sign.

Tools for Chip Carving

Chip carving requires carefully practiced and well-developed skill to enable the wood carver to execute a clean and attractive cutting. Normally the tools used are a hooknosed cutting knife and a skewed or flat stab knife; soft, featureless timber generally produces best results **(8-4)**.

8-4 A hook-nosed knife is used for cutting the patterns; the flat stab knife is used for cutting in clean shadow lines in the bottoms of those cuts. These are the two basic and traditional tools of the chip carver; however, regular carving tools can also be used, particularly the skew.

You can also undertake chip carving with ordinary knives and woodcarving tools chosen to suit the pattern; so if you don't have or can't purchase knives like those in the illustration, try skews and gouges as an alternative. Large lettering, like that shown earlier in **8-1**, might be more easily done with a combination of chip-carving knives and regular gouges. There are no rules! But as you develop different ideas, you will most likely want to use the typical chip-cutting and stab knives as a matter of course.

8-5 Your physical comfort is vital for successful chip carving. Accuracy is a necessity for well-cut accurate lines and curves, and relaxed comfort is essential to achieve this.

8-6 Notice how the thumb is used for control and to give pulling strength for drawing the tool through the wood. The thumb is the strongest finger in the hand and can be used to great advantage with tool handling. You will notice that the more you carve, the stronger your hands will become, and this in turn will give you greater dexterity and control.

8-7 The stab knife is used by pushing the end of the blade into the bottoms of cuts to help make them clean, and to place, if necessary, a cut in the bottom of the groove so that a shadow line is introduced.

HOLDING THE CHIP-CARVING KNIVES

As we said right back at the beginning of this book, the only rule for carving is comfort—both physical and mental comfort. So, the only rule about holding the specialty chip-carving knives described in the sidebar on the opposite page is that you are comfortable—and safe. A posture that for most of us will be the most comfortable is shown in **8-5**. The board for the pattern is held in the left hand if you are right-handed; if it is large, rest it on your knee while sitting. As with all carving, tool control is the key, and this can best be achieved only when comfort is there. The use of the cutting knife is shown in **8-6** and the stab knife in **8-7**.

DRAWING THE PATTERN

See the sidebar to the right on designs for chip carving. Now, let's draw our pattern. The pattern is drawn on the wood in solid form in **8-8**. An alternative method is shown in **8-9**. This may be preferred because it has a centerline that can be used as a focus for determining the depth of the cut you want to make. Once you have a depth of cut for your knife in mind, use this centerline for aiming the tip of the blade accordingly.

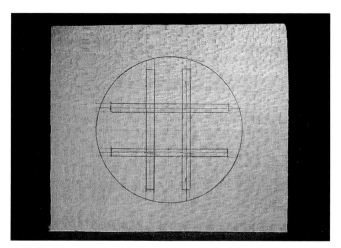

8-9 Careful measuring is needed to ensure the lines are at right angles (or whichever angle you choose) and to ensure that the cuts are the same width. Make sure the centerlines are in the center, because if they aren't, it will be impossible to get your cuts looking right—unless, of course, they are intended to be off center.

Designs for Chip Carving

As with all art, chip-carving designs may be as simple or as complex as you want to make them. Complexity is not necessarily the prerequisite for beauty; indeed, simplicity is often the more attractive proposition. While traditional chip carving is made up of geometric patterns, free-form is also very popular.

8-8 The pattern we have chosen is the dollar sign. It combines straight lines, curves, and basic chips. This can be carved equally easily with the traditional chip-carving cutting and stab knives or with your skew chisel from your standard carving tool collection.

Free-form design is really drawing a picture with incised lines. For our exercise, we will stay with the more traditional approach; however, we will choose as our subject something a little more close to our hearts than geometry, as seen above in **8-8**.

8-10 *The development of a high skill level for chip carving requires a lot of practice. Make yourself several disposable practice boards that you can use on both sides. Make them from different timbers so you can experience how they cut.*

Keeping Your Chip-Carving Knives Sharp

If you purchase top-quality chip-carving knives, and you use only softer woods such as basswood, your knives will stay sharp for a considerable time. Before you use a slip stone, however, take a good look at the bevel configuration on the cutting edges. In most cases, the blades will be thin in cross section, and the bevels will be quite short. Try to maintain the original bevel shapes unless you are certain that an alternative will do

8-11 *The push knife is being sharpened with the slip stone. Lay it flat on its back to remove any burr, after sharpening the bevel on the top side. The hook-nosed knife is sharpened the same way.*

a better job. Certainly experiment, but be prepared to reinstate the original if necessary (**8-11**). Your knife should cut the basswood like a razor, with no scratching or tearing visible. If your knife is not really sharp, tool control will be difficult.

FIRST CUTS

Once you have organized a design or two, it is time to make your practice board (**8-10**). In these illustrations we are using basswood (linden). It is soft, close-grained, has no figure that will interfere with the patterns, and cuts cleanly and efficiently. A good thickness for a practice board is about ½ inch. It is comfortable to hold and will not break. The surface needs to be smooth, so use dressed timber. If you need to sand it, which should not really be necessary, make absolutely certain there is no sanding grit left in the wood, as it will ruin your sharp knife blade. See the sidebar opposite and **8-11** about keeping your knives sharp.

Cut a few practice boards, because the skills needed to make effective chip carving can only be learned by practice. The basis of the *chip cut* is shown in **8-12**. Once you are comfortable, and you are holding your board stable, press the tip of your hook-nosed knife into the wood so that it makes a V cut. The center of the V (that is, the tip of the knife blade) should be directly below the centerline of the cut. Make the same cut on each side of the triangle, and you should have the waste pop out to form an inverted pyramid. Practice this over and over and over, along with some straight-line cuts (**8-13**) and you are well on the way to some exciting times as a chip carver! It is most likely that you will need to go over your cuts until they are clean and even.

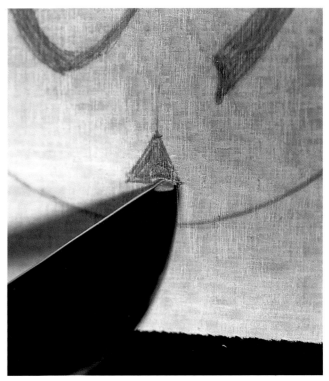

8-12 Start practicing with an equilateral triangle with sides ¼ inch long. Don't start too large to begin with, as you might find it too difficult to achieve clean cuts, and each time you recut them, there is further opportunity to make it uneven. Point the tip of the knife toward the center of the triangle, and press it firmly into the wood so that an inverted pyramid is formed. Repeat this three times and, if each cut is accurate, the waste will pop out.

8-13 Practice straight-line cutting, but don't make the width too great (⅛ inch is perfect), and don't cut too deeply to start (¹/₁₆ inch is enough).

EXECUTING THE CHIP-CARVING DESIGN

The same principles that we have been discussing are applicable to all the chip-carving designs you will ever do. Experimentation is the key to success; when experimentation is combined with practiced skill, many very attractive designs can be achieved. Once you have drawn in your pattern as shown earlier in **8-8**, continue with the following sequence.

Make the straight cuts first (**8-14**). They are easiest to do, and, when you have successfully completed them, you will have the confidence to do the curves.

Control while cutting the curves is always the challenge. The curve we have chosen has a deliberately tapered shape, because it is more difficult to get them to have parallel sides (**8-15**). Make sure you cut the ends of the curved parts first, just the same as for the straight lines. This also helps stop the wood from tearing beyond the pattern.

If you want to cut your dollar sign into a circle (you could use a scroll saw or a band saw) do this before you sand. This is because once you have sanded the drawn circle off, it will be very difficult to get it positioned in the right place again (**8-16**).

8-14 Cut the end in first, simply by pushing the knife into the wood as with the triangle you practiced earlier. This ensures that once the side cuts are completed the waste will pop out neatly. You could make these end cuts vertical, or slope them in at the same angle as the sides. For the curved cuts, it may be necessary to make one cut and then do a completing or tidying-up cut. This is not desirable, as it is always better to do it in one go; however, with care it will look as though this was in fact done.

8-15 For curves, you will need to manipulate the board and the knife so that you cut accurately around the pencil mark. This will require greater control than you have had to use so far, so it is understandable if it takes a little longer to master. Your initial cuts will look a little untidy like this, but soon you will notice a rapid improvement.

8-16 Cut in the two decorative triangles on either side of the dollar sign if you did not do it at the beginning (there is no special order in which to do things). Use the push knife to clean up the bottoms of the grooves. The flat end of the blade will put in place clean shadow lines. If you wish, sand the surface with a very fine (say, 400-grade grit) sandpaper, making sure to use a sanding block (an offcut of wood is adequate) to keep the surface quite flat. If the edges of the dollar sign are cleanly and evenly cut, sanding will ensure a sharp edge that will look smart.

FINISHING

For items that will not be in the weather (such as this piece or internal or undercover exterior signs like the one shown earlier in **8-2**) an oiled finish may be best. Tung oil is an excellent choice; however, most nut oils are very satisfactory. Orange oil is another alternative.

Exterior signage (such as the one in **8-1**) should be finished with appropriate weather-resistant surface treatments. Choose a weatherproof polyurethane finish with an added ultraviolet-light filter (sunscreen), which will significantly reduce oxidation of the wood and help it maintain its natural color.

You could use this medallion design for a drink coaster, or you could make a hole in the top and use it as a pendant (**8-17**).

8-17 The finished medallion.

Chapter Nine

DOUBLE JEOPARDY
Venturing into Pierced Relief

Pierced relief is, as the name suggests, simply relief carving with holes through it. It is a very decorative form of carving appropriate for screens, such as the small decorative rosewood screen above that might be used to decorate a tabletop with flowers or a candle behind for lighting effect. Pierced carving can also be incorporated into many designs such as those for music stands, bookends, and fancy box lids such as those for potpourri.

APPLICATIONS OF PIERCED RELIEF

Pierced-relief carving designs take many forms. The edges might be free-form arabesque like the screen on the opposite page, or the design might incorporate a frame-like border as an integral part of the pattern, as in the music stand in **9-1**. Other designs may have a definitive frame, as in the composition in **9-2**. A pattern that does not have a border should not have any parts protruding that might get caught and break off, or, in the case of a music stand, catch the music pages.

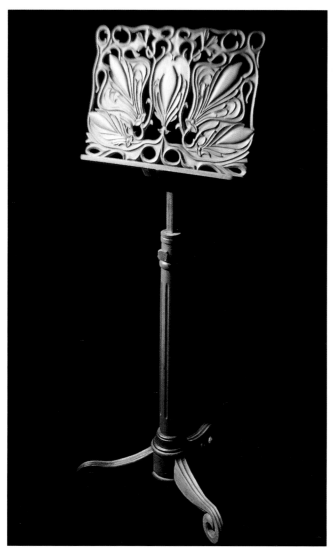

9-1 *Pierced relief is a very attractive proposition for furniture such as music stands.*

Designing a Pierced Relief

It is very important when designing a pierced relief that the junction points of the pattern, either with other parts of the carving itself and/or any framing, are strong enough and frequent enough to ensure the general strength of the work. Parts of the design that come to points or very small dimensions should not be used as connecting points.

It is equally important that the work is not subject to any excessive stress that may crack it. For this reason, the clown design for your first attempt is completed using only a bench hook, the carving being held still by your hand or wrist resting on it while using the tools. Avoid placing the work in jaw-type clamps that may squeeze it. If you do use G clamps, make sure that the piece is not warped too much and that the clamping surface is flat, with no wood chips on it; otherwise you may crack it. If there is a warp, try steaming the wood with a steam iron, wet cloth, and hot water, and clamping it flat while it is still wet and warm.

9-2 *"Butterflies" is a particularly fun carving. The butterflies are carved in pierced relief on a separate sheet of timber (in this case silver ash) and then mounted in a frame of pink myrtle, with a backboard in the same. The backboard is about ½ inch from the butterflies, encouraging some strong shadow activity behind them.*

Wood for Pierced Carving

For most situations, the wood should:

Be reasonably strong so that it will not be too weak once the pattern is cut;

Be of a species that doesn't split or fracture easily, particularly for finer work;

Not be coarse and grainy; otherwise the edges may chip and the pattern may easily break;

Be stable and weather resistant if it is for external use, such as for architectural decoration (e.g., corner brackets or gable ends).

Good examples are American black walnut, European oak (American white oak is a bit too tough and stringy), and South American (Honduran) mahogany.

A Note on Cutting Blades

Whether you are using a machine tool such as a scroll saw, or a handheld fret or coping saw, it is important to test different cutting blades. Some blades will cut quite coarsely, and this will leave an unattractive edge on your work. Machine scroll-saw blades are manufactured in different widths, narrower widths being more suitable to finer and more delicate patterns.

One of the best styles of blade is known as a *skip-tooth blade*. These blades have every third tooth missing; this allows for better dust removal and a finer, cleaner cut. Often, the skip-tooth blade is also ground in its manufacturing process rather than pressed; this means that the blade is more accurate and cuts more cleanly, because both faces of the teeth are uniformly set.

SUITABLE WOOD FOR PIERCED CARVING

Choosing wood for pierced carving projects must be carefully thought through; as in every other case where there might be doubt, testing should be part of the routine, as described in the sidebar on the opposite page. The final choice of wood will be made with regard to the design and its purpose; so a wood for a pierced box lid may be quite different from a wood for a fancy pierced external architectural bracket.

Tools for Pierced Carving

Pierced carving is in effect carved fretwork; you will need a fretsaw, a coping saw, or an electric-powered scroll saw for the pattern cutting, and a power drill and bit to make holes to allow access for the cutting blade to fit into the wood (**9-3**).

9-3 An electric-powered scroll saw is best for this kind of work; however, with patience the same effect can be achieved with a fretsaw or coping saw.

A Simple Suitability Test for Wood for Pierced Work

The making of this peg-board illustrates a way to test wood that, while usable for this peg board, is not suited to detailed pierced carving. The test requires only one hole.

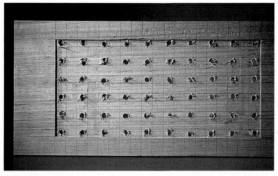

9-4 Broken wood caused by a drill may indicate unsuitability for pierced relief. Check that the drill is sharp and not too much pressure is applied during drilling. A second piece of wood under the exit hole may also stop tearing out of the wood.

Drill a single ⅛-inch (3mm) hole through the wood. If your drill is reasonably new and therefore sharp, and tear-out occurs when the drill exits the wood as in **9-4**, the wood may not be suitable.

Cut down through the end grain on the end of a board using an almost flat small gouge as shown in **9-5**. Check for two aspects:

9-5 Cut through the end grain with an almost flat gouge. If it is completely flat, the corners or shoulders of the tool will cause tearing.

Make sure the end grain, when you cut vertically down through it, doesn't squash or break up, as shown in **9-6**.

Make sure that the long grain doesn't break away or appear too stringy, as shown in **9-7**.

9-6 The red arrowheads indicate where the grain in this ash has fractured and broken away because the wood is too brittle, unsuitable for end-grain cutting.

9-7 The stringy broken grain in this piece of ash indicates the wood is too weak; this kind of fracturing might interfere with the pattern.

A CARVING PROJECT USING PIERCED RELIEF

For our project with pierced relief we will have some fun making a clown for the kitchen table using the pattern in **9-8**. We will use a piece of South American (Honduran) mahogany, dressed to 8 inches × 8 inches × ⅜ inch thick (200mm × 200mm × 10mm). You can alter it to any size you wish; however, ⅜ inch (10mm) is about as thin as is safe for a first time around.

If you decide to make your clown larger than 8 inches by 8 inches, it is possible that the thin piece may warp a little, especially after it is pierced. This will depend on the natural stresses in the wood and the weather. If it does warp, it should be relatively easy to fix by gluing a long square piece of wood along the bottom of the carving This piece will double as a base to support it standing upright. If it doesn't warp after cutting or during carving, gluing such a piece in place for the base will prevent its happening in the future.

All the carving for the clown is done on a home-made bench hook; there is no need for clamps of any kind. If you choose your wood carefully, there is no need for a mallet either. Using a harder wood that

9-8 Enlarge the pattern so that it will cover an 8-inch-square starting block, and then copy the pattern onto your wood. A thickness of about ⅜ inch (10mm) in a straight-grained, medium-density wood, such as South American (Honduran) mahogany, is perfect.

needs a mallet for power and control may in fact be a disadvantage as it may cause too much jarring and crack the frame or the carving, particularly at the junctions of the clown and the frame.

The carving for the clown is relatively simple. You do need to be careful, since you will carve it from both sides; you can't afford to "over-carve" one side or the other. This means that you will need to either draw in with your pencil, or estimate while you carve, a midline between the two faces (the front and the back). As you carve in from each face, don't go beyond this midline. The edge at the midline needn't necessarily be "sharp," such as where the two carved faces meet, but can be slightly rounded. You can decide this as you progress—completing whichever look you prefer.

The first step is to draw on your pattern, and cut out the waste (**9-9**).

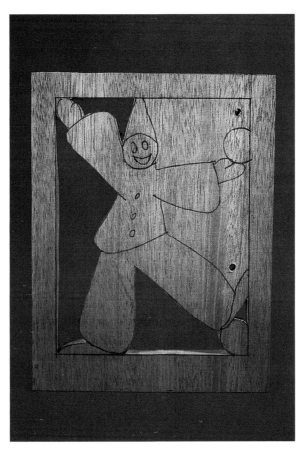

9-9 This cutout has been done with a scroll saw. The holes drilled before cutting out the waste are to allow access for the blade. The importance of having strong anchor points where the pattern meets the frame will become very clear now.

Working with Complex Pierced Work

The pierced reliefs seen on the opening page of this chapter and in **9-2** and **9-3** are made in the same way as we are making this clown design, except for a few extra considerations. Additional care needs to be exercised to prevent cracking; the design needs to be audited to ensure strength where it is needed most; there are some additional tools for cutting some of the concave parts; and the holding device needs to be quite different.

Avoid wherever possible clamping or using jaw-type devices, which may place excessive pressure on weaker places, breaking them. It is best to make a pegboard or similar device that can be specifically designed for the piece. The making of a snug-fitting holding device is worth taking the time to do. Often we are too anxious to get carving; we begin and persist with ill-fitting or inadequate devices that, in the end, cause frustration and possibly substantial damage.

If you are using an existing pegboard, one solution to a loose-fitting arrangement of the pegs is to have on hand a few different-sized wedges that can be gently tapped into place to make a firm fit. This way there is no need to continually drill more holes. The wedges are easy to remove so the carving can be taken out.

MARKING IN THE DETAILS

When the cutting out is complete, use your V tool to mark in the lines around the ankles, belt line, hands, and face (**9-10**). Don't cut in too deep, as you will only be using these lines as a guide for further shaping. Since the wood is to become quite thin in places, be careful as you handle the piece while carving and shaping that you not apply too much pressure, otherwise you might inadvertently crack it.

On the reverse side, you can draw in with a pencil the corresponding head, hands, belt line, and feet. Draw in some hair on the back of the head, which can later be cut in with the V tool or small fluter.

CARVING SEQUENCE

All of the shaping can be done with a ¼-inch (6mm) almost flat gouge, together with a ½-inch (13mm) almost flat gouge and a ⅜-inch (10mm) skew. Use a ¹⁄₃₂-inch (1mm) fluter or a small V tool for the eyes and buttons, and cut in the mouth with your ¼-inch gouge or a more curved fluter.

Shape the front and then the back (**9-11, 9-12**) alternating to keep things even and help prevent cutting too deeply in any one place (**9-13, 9-14**). Your bench hook is a convenient holding device for this kind of work where you need to continuously move the carving around and turn it over.

9-10 Mark in the key lines with your V tool. Avoid cutting too deeply as you might crack the wood. Leave the details of the eyes, mouth, and buttons until the very end. It is best not to try to do these with a V tool but rather with a small fluter.

9-11 *Alternate between carving the front . . .*

9-12 *. . . and the back.*

9-13 *Refine the front . . .*

9-14 *. . . and the back.*

Leave some parts of the carving the original thickness of the wood so they can act as a support for the remainder as you carve it (**9-15**, **9-16**). Otherwise the wood will flex under pressure and may crack.

An alternative to your bench hook for holding your work is a pegboard. This is easy to make and very versatile (one is being made in the sidebar on page 115). The pegboard is used with some wedges and packing pieces, secured against the edge of the workbench with a cleat like your bench hook, and clamped in place with a G clamp, if necessary, to stop it from moving around, particularly if you are using a mallet.

FINISHING

The completed clown in **9-17** has been finished with some fine sandpaper (220 grit), and then rubbed with furniture wax.

9-15 *Some parts of the carving should remain essentially at the original thickness to help support the integrity of the wood. Shaping the front some more and alternate to the back so that the overall level of carving is kept the same.*

9-16 *Be careful when you are handling the carving not to put too much pressure on any point or you might accidently crack the piece. Shape the back to keep its progress equivalent to that of the front.*

9-17 The finished pierced-relief carving was finished with fine sandpaper and then rubbed with furniture wax.

Chapter Ten

FINER FURNITURE
Extending Relief Carving to Furniture Decoration

For many of us there is an ambition to be able to make good quality, long-lasting furniture for our home, or a simple but useful item that is also decorative. Whatever the case, being able to place some decorative carving on what we make might give us great satisfaction and at the same time make a worthwhile attractive addition to the piece.

CONSIDERATIONS IN CARVING FOR FURNITURE

The principles of carving for furniture are the same as for the relief carving we did for the leaf bowl. However, there are some additional points that need to be addressed in the case of carving for furniture. Like most things that are for practical use rather than purely decorative use, there will always be some catches.

How the Furniture Is to Be Used

The design needs to take into consideration the use the furniture will be put to. Raised parts are inappropriate for chair backs, for example, where the carving needs to be smooth and level with the surface so it will not get caught on clothing. Likewise, fancy work on chair and table legs needs to be designed to take into consideration the chances of being knocked by vacuum cleaners and shoes.

The greater the amount and depth of detail in the carving the greater the chances of its collecting dust. If the piece is to be used in a potentially high dust environment, the simpler the carving the better from a maintenance point of view.

Suitability of Wood for Carving

Many of the woods that are good for furniture making are difficult and inappropriate for carving. This does not mean they can't be carved, but it does mean that the design and the tools need to be chosen to make the carving feasible. Often a good furniture timber will be too tough or stringy for carving, but will respond well to machine tools and some hand planes. It is important before embarking on the project to test the wood with some carving tools to make sure you are happy with its suitability for what you want to carve.

Carving on a Project You Are Building

If you are planning to place some carving on some components of furniture you are making, it is important to allow enough wood for the carving in the design of the component. It may be that you need to build into the component design some extra wood in a raised-up area to accommodate the carving. As an alternative, it is often easier to do the carving separately, and glue it in place later.

Where to Start Carving for Furniture

With all of these things in mind, don't let any of it stop you from giving it a try. It's just that if we think about these things up front, then we are more likely to have a result that brings us great pleasure later on. If you would like to make something, but are not quite sure what, here are some ideas:

> Bookends
>
> Magazine rack
>
> Book reading rack or tray
>
> Wall bracket for a potted plant
>
> Coffeepot stand
>
> Key rack
>
> Coat rack

Take a look around your home, or flip through some magazines. Somewhere there will be the idea just waiting for you to put into practice.

Types of Finish

A high-gloss synthetic surface on the furniture may be necessary for maintenance reasons, but it makes the piece inappropriate for carving. Decorative carving often looks ugly with a high-gloss finish, as there is too much light reflection, and it can become gaudy. Think carefully before using high gloss on your work.

Effects of Carving Furniture

The act of carving reduces the volume of wood, and this may cause weakness in it, which will be inappropriate for furniture. A carved tabletop may become too thin for practical use, for example. Careful planning is needed with the preparation of the wood stock and the application of the design to it.

The act of carving also increases the exposed surface area on the side where the carving is. This may mean that in some environments the wood will warp or cup. For example, if the carving is for a large panel, it may be necessary to reinforce it.

A DESIGN TO START WITH FOR FURNITURE

The pattern we are going to carve can be adapted for any of the items suggested in the sidebar on "Where to Start." You might have to alter the proportions a little, or duplicate some parts, but one way or another it can be adapted (**10-1**).

Transferring the Pattern to the Wood

We will use some Honduran mahogany for our carving. It is a good furniture wood, easy to carve and generally easy to purchase. Transfer your pattern to the wood (**10-2**), in a similar manner as you did for the top view of the leaf bowl that we carved in Chapter 3, "What a Relief!" Use a dark colored pencil to go over the pattern to make it easier to see.

10-1 Our flower and leaf design has no raised (protruding) parts, so it is ideal for furniture items of all kinds. If you want to place it on a rectangular panel for a magazine rack, for example, simply duplicate the sprig of leaves in mirror image on the left-hand side. Depending on the proportions, you may need to reposition the sprig of leaves so it is lying flatter on the wood. Photocopy the pattern to the size you want, or redraw it by hand.

10-2 For best copying results, make sure the surface of the wood is planed cleanly. Use a ballpoint pen rather than a pencil for transferring the pattern when using carbonized paper, as a pencil will probably tear through the paper. To make it easier to see, go back over the tracing with a very-fine-tipped felt pen, testing first on the back of the wood to make sure the ink doesn't run in the grain of the wood.

CARVING SEQUENCE

To successfully create your leaf design, follow the sequence **10-3** through **10-5**.

Cut around the pattern with a V tool to mark it into the wood, as shown near the label "1" in **10-3**.

With a small, reasonably flat gouge, set in the pattern by roughing out the waste so that you achieve a vertical edge around the entire pattern, as shown near the label "2" around the outside of the flower. You will need to decide whether you want to recess the pattern into the wood as it is here, or whether you want to remove all the background as it is at area "3," as labeled in photo **10-3**. If you want the background removed entirely, use a gouge that is very flat but not absolutely. A flat carpenter's chisel, for example, will leave "tram-tracks" where the corners dig into the surface.

The leaf, labeled "4" in **10-3**, in between the flower and the next leaf should be cut in about half the depth of the flower. Shape the leaf as best you can before removing the narrow waste around it just above the number "5". This waste between the stalks, areas "1" and "5," is tricky, and, if great care is not taken, the

Tools for Carving Furniture

For this flower and leaf carving you will need at least the tools described in Appendix 3, "Essential Tools for the Projects & How to Hold Them." When you decide to do more detailed relief carving or carve in the round for furniture then you may find that you need additional tools beyond the basic ones, for instance, those suitable for sculptural carving.

stalks will break away. To help prevent this, reduce the height first to the thickness of the finished stalks, then redraw them on and carefully cut around them, avoiding placing any pressure in toward them.

Before you do anything to the petals, such as label "6" in **10-3**, you will need to decide whether you want them concave or convex and whether they are all the same height or whether some should appear to tuck in under others.

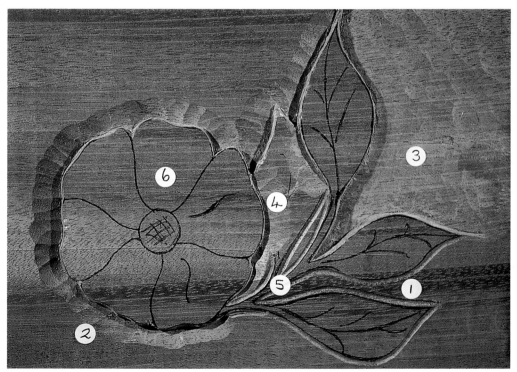

10-3 As the carving progresses, you will need to make decisions along the way. The labels are also referred to in the text. Label "1" shows the cutting in of the design with a V tool. Label "2" shows roughing out the waste to achieve a vertical edge. Label "3" marks the background, which requires a decision about its treatment. Label "4" shows the lowering of a leaf and "5" marks the tricky area of stems and narrow waste. Label "6" marks a petal to remind us to think through how they should look before continuing to carve.

To get things going, cut away the edges of one of the petals, as shown by label "7" in **10-4**. Don't cut too deeply at first, until you work out what you want the shape to be.

Mark with your pen some instructions to yourself. Use arrowheads to indicate the direction in which you think the petals should curve, as shown by label "8" in **10-4**.

You will need to decide whether you want these leaves to be convex or concave. From an artistic point of view, don't make them all the same. Make one or two convex, and the others concave, or make them partly convex and concave. We are trying to create shadows, so the more "movement" over the surface the more likely this is going to occur.

Continue to reduce the height of the background near the stalks and leaves and start to shape the tops of the leaves, as shown near label "9" in **10-4**.

Once you have reduced the height of the wood where the stalks are, it is time to carefully cut them in, as shown near label "10." Use a tool that is ⅛ inch or less wide to get into these small places, working carefully and cleanly.

All the background is now removed, as shown near label "11" in **10-5**. You will see from the pattern, as we said at the beginning, that nothing is protruding to make a hazard for clothing to get caught on, or for vacuum cleaners to knock off. This is a very important design consideration. When you are removing the background, it is likely that the wood will tear if the grain is "cranky" or you are cutting against it. If this happens, change the cutting direction until you find one that is not going to cause a broken surface. It may be necessary to change direction frequently. For this reason it is very convenient to be somewhat ambidextrous in your carving technique.

The tips of the leaves are a fragile area, as shown near label "12." Once you have cut the waste away from one side, there is no wood left to support the tip on that side, so as you cut the wood away from the other side if you place undue pressure on the tip it will break off. Be circumspect, placing as much of the pressure from the tool away from the tip. Cutting along the side of the leaf rather that in toward it will help, but you will need to ensure your vertical cut (the stop cut) is clean and the correct depth.

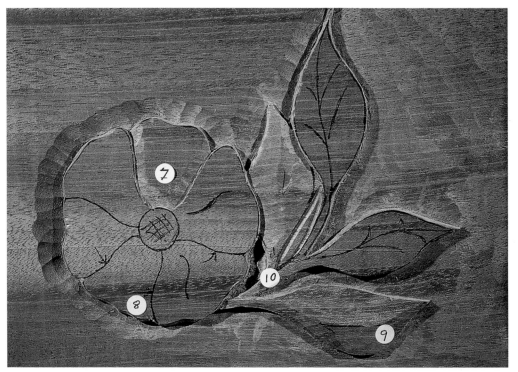

10-4 *Label "7" shows the start of cutting away of one of the petals. One way to mark the petals with instructions to yourself on how to carve them is shown near label "8." Beginning to shape the top of a leaf and reducing more of the background is shown near label "9." Label "10" marks the delicate stalk area that is ready to be cut in.*

The leaf below label "13" and the one above we have elected to cut concave. This makes for good shadow activity. Bring the concavity right to the edge of the leaf, so there are no flat areas around it.

On two of the petals we have included a small fold, for added interest, as shown near label "14" and the petal below. Cut these in with your gouge. They increase the shadow activity, depending on where the light is coming from, as can be seen in the one on the bottom petal.

FINAL DETAILS

Finally, clean up the surface of any areas that you want to have a smooth appearance, as shown for the petal labeled "15," and chamfer the edges.

Finishing with Chamfered Edges

It is a good idea for furniture patterns like these to chamfer the edges. Chamfering is simply the cutting of a slight bevel on what would otherwise be sharp edges. This reduces the likelihood that edges will break away with use, and it enhances the shadow activity of the pattern, making it more interesting.

Use your skew to chamfer the edges, making sure your skew is very sharp so that there is no tearing or chipping.

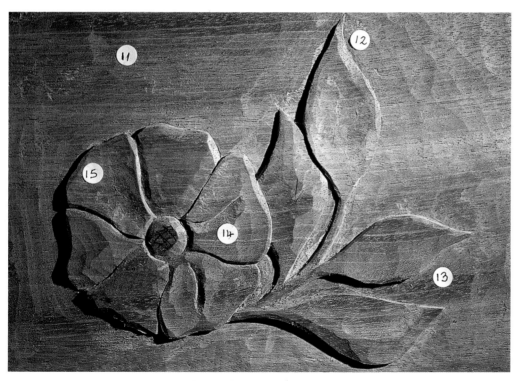

10-5 All of the background is removed, as marked by label "11." Care must be taken around the fragile tips of the leaves, such as near label "12." Label "13" draws our attention to the treatment of the leaves above and below. A gouge has been used to create a small fold in the petal marked by label "14" and the one below. Label "15" marks the finishing of a petal with chamfered edges.

Chapter Eleven

JUST PICTURE IT!
Photography for Woodcarvers

Some of the most important tools we have for developing a carving are the various means we use to picture our subject and our intended results. Sketches, drawings, and models are one set of tools. But for many of us, photography is appealing and serves as a viable option to drawing. Photography is also important for recording our work and as an aid to seeing the piece we are creating. We can use lighting as a tool to highlight the details in our work. Indeed, for relief carving itself shadows are precisely what we are trying to create, so recording relief carvings photographically with the right shadow can be very beneficial.

Photography is an important tool we can use to develop our carvings and record our work. In Chapter 5, "Dreaming of Drawing?" we took a look at some of the ways we can hone our skills for drawing subjects we would like to carve in the future. Even for those whose drawing skills are well developed, photography can be a significant tool for carving. Photography is particularly useful for recording animal subjects, where the detail is often (and understandably) beyond our sketching ability, and it is virtually essential for recording human anatomy especially if we want to create a bust as discussed in Chapter 13, "Let's Face It." In this chapter we discuss many of the aspects of photography that will affect our results.

KEEPING YOUR EQUIPMENT SIMPLE

As anyone involved with photography at an amateur level has experienced, there is an enormous variety of photographic equipment available at prices ranging from affordable to most to affordable to few. To keep the discussion within the realms of practicality for the average hobby photographer, the equipment we will discuss will be confined to basics. Nothing used will have restricted availability to most consumers.

DIGITAL & CONVENTIONAL FILM MEDIA

There is great appeal in the potential use of digital photography as the ease and flexibility of the medium has become more apparent. I will not discuss the technical aspects of digital photography, leaving that to the user's guides that accompany such cameras. Since conventional film photography is still the most widely used medium, I will discuss some of its technical considera-

Does Lighting Matter?

If you have ever been game hunting or had experience in the military, you will perhaps know a little about camouflage. In essence, the requirements for our photography for recording carvings are the reverse of the requirements for camouflage. What we need to achieve are photographs that record as much of the detail as possible. We need to be less concerned with panoramic views and scenery and more with light direction, shadows, focus, and close-up detail. Camouflage is about concealing detail; our photography needs to reveal as much as possible.

To achieve what we need, it is very important to understand the effects of lighting on our subject matter. We will look at the key elements in turn under "Elements of Lighting.."

tions over which the user has some control. But, with the exception of the comments about film, just about everything else mentioned applies equally to digital as to conventional film photography.

Conventional 35mm Film Cameras

We will compare results from two styles of camera—the popular compact or "point-and-shoot," and the traditional single-lens reflex (SLR) style. All the film will be 35mm for color prints (the most practical reference material) in standard postcard size.

What Are We Trying to Photograph?

It is important to note that some of the aspects of our photography for carving are quite different from the kinds of photography that we might be used to doing. If we normally dabble in holiday snapshots we will find that the kinds of things we do for that sort of photography may not be nearly satisfactory enough for our needs for photographing carvings, or subjects we might want to carve.

ELEMENTS OF LIGHTING

Important elements of lighting include reflection, shadow, and treatment of the background.

Lighting & Reflection

Shiny surfaces reflect greater amounts of more concentrated light than duller surfaces. *Shine* or *reflection*, while making the presence of an object more obvious, tends to obscure detail. This is very important if you are photographing a shiny object with a flash (**11-1**). Photographing shiny objects is best done with a diffused light rather than a concentrated one. If you can't use a floodlight that will make light more generalized than your flash, then be prepared to have photos with shiny areas that may require detail recording by sketching. If you know you are going to be in an environment, such as an exhibition, where lighting is low and you think the use of a flash may be necessary, choose a film with a high film speed (see the sidebar "Which Film?"), which may not always need the flash.

Lighting & Shadow

Shadows are often one of the best ways of highlighting detail, but they can also be one of the things that can cause distortion and confusion of the very detail we want to highlight. Indeed, for relief carving itself shadows are precisely what we are trying to create, so recording relief carvings photographically with the right shadow can be very beneficial.

11-2 This photograph has a good balance of shadow, showing off the carving's detail to good effect and making it easy to see. The lighting arrangement is shown in 11-3.

11-1 Use of a flash can cause high reflection that may obliterate the very detail you are trying to record.

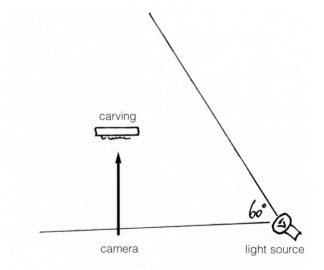

carving

camera

light source

60°

11-3 This is a plan view of the lighting arrangement for 11-2. The light has a 60-degree arc and is positioned to create short, crisp shadows. The camera is at the bottom facing the carving.

Too much shadow will hide detail, and not enough may also hide or confuse it. These variations are shown in **11-2** through **11-7**. If you are unable to use artificial light to create some shadows, then sunlight is your only option. The best sunlight for this is in the morning and afternoon, when the sun is lower in the sky and casts some shadows. But too early in the morning and too late in the afternoon should probably be avoided, depending on time of year and your latitude, since at these times of day the shadows will be longest. During the middle of the day, when the sun appears highest in the sky, the shadows will be their shortest.

11-4 This photograph has shadows that are too long and tend to darken the overall view, hiding detail. The lighting arrangement is shown in 11-5.

11-6 This photograph has almost no shadows, making some of the detail impossible to easily see, if at all. When planning your photograph, some shadow is mostly better than no shadow.

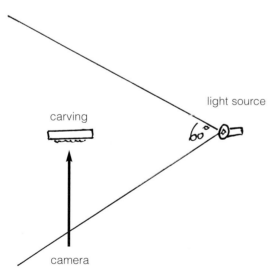

11-5 This is a plan view of the lighting arrangement for 11-4. The light is positioned too square on, making shadows that are too long. The camera is at the bottom facing the carving, thus at 90 degrees to the light source.

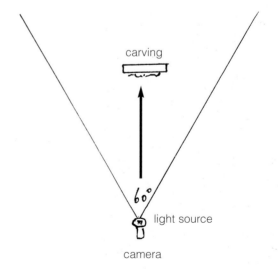

11-7 This is a plan view of the lighting arrangement for 11-6. Light directly in front of the subject will tend to reduce shadows. For outdoor photographs morning or afternoon light will cast shadows, and the midday sun will minimize them. The camera is at the bottom at the same location as the light, facing the carving.

Lighting, Silhouette & Background Color

Silhouette is the result of lighting and color contrasts that cause shape to be easily seen. Silhouette is an excellent phenomenon to use for the recording of profiles for carvings in the round.

Silhouette can be the result of using light to cause contrast, or by using color to the same effect. It is easier to use color, but if you can combine the two, then this is better still. If you want to record your family pet so you can carve or model it, some photographs using shadow to highlight the positioning of some of the detail are very useful, and, if you supplement these with some shots highlighting the silhouette, then you are even better off.

Do this by photographing the pet on or in front of a highly contrasting color background. A colored rug, some paper, a painted wall as a backdrop are some ideas. Avoid irregular backgrounds such as multi-colored flowerbeds or lots of shrubs with dappled light and so on. Your pet might actually blend into them! This effect is seen in **11-8** and **11-9**, with a dramatic foliage demonstration.

11-8 *The background hides some of the important details that you need to ensure the right shape of the leaf.*

11-9 *Introducing a contrasting color makes the detail much easier to see.*

USING DIFFERENT KINDS OF LIGHT

One of the first things we need to become aware of is that not all sources of light will produce the same image, and different lights actually have different colors to them that can make a particular film unsatisfactory.

Natural Sunlight

We have already mentioned sunlight and shadow creation under the heading "Lighting & Shadow." One of the great advantages (and it can also be a great disadvantage) of sunlight is that it will show every small imperfection imaginable. If sunlight is not diffused, such as by cloud cover, it can be a very unforgiving lighting medium. To test this statement, simply take a carving you are working on from your workshop out into daylight. If you have soft or low-level or fluorescent lighting in your workshop, you will immediately see all the mistakes, scratches, chips, and so on that you probably cannot normally see. You may well be horrified!

The trouble with sunlight is, of course, that it is unpredictable, and it moves all the time, making any photographic session using it for shadows a little difficult. Another warning is that if you are planning a photo session in your garden using sunlight, be very sure that trees and shrubs will not cast unexpected shadows at the wrong time. Unless you are sure of it, sunlight can be a frustrating medium to plan by.

Sunlight can also be very bright and cause a lot of glare. It may be necessary to avoid white cloth backdrops or light-colored painted walls. The light reflecting from these may interfere with your camera's light meter readings in relation to the light reflected from the subject itself. If the reflected light from a backdrop is too bright, your subject may be significantly underexposed and, chances are, not much detail will be visible at all.

Household Reading Lights

To the unsuspecting photographer, all household reading lights are assumed to be the same. Unfortunately, they are not; the results in your photography can vary from success to disaster.

The light sources that we use have a technical specification known as *color temperature*. The different color temperatures of different light sources literally emit different colors to one another.

Which Camera?

As mentioned earlier, while you may find that digital photography is the way you want to go, here we will compare some choices that can be made for conventional 35mm film equipment.

A 35mm SLR (single-lens reflex) camera will offer the greatest flexibility as regards film speeds, lenses, filters, and other accessories.

A compact "point-and-shoot" camera may not offer a satisfactory close-up range. It is important to check the specifications as additional close-up lenses or lens adaptors may not be available. Close-up photography is called *macrophotography*.

Ensure the camera you purchase is able to use higher-speed films. At least 400 ISO is advisable for conditions of low-level light.

Check the specifications for the flash to ensure that it is suitable for close-up work. The camera may not be able to adjust the light output for shorter-distance photography.

While a basic SLR camera might be the same price as a compact camera, be aware that the accessories for the SLR may price it out of reach.

A macro lens is normally unsuitable for general photography, so that the price of an additional "regular" lens needs to be ascertained as well.

On the next page we will see some of the effects of the different colors of tungsten halogen lights and flourescent lighting on photography. The important point to remember is that each different variety of light source may emit a different color; the film you place in your camera may not be able to satisfactorily reproduce the color so that it looks natural. Be sure you also consult the sidebar "Which Film?" on the next page.

Which Film?

The film you choose will depend on a number of factors; here are some pointers that may help your choice:

Color prints are the most convenient archival method and will give very crisp, clear detail. Color transparencies (slides) are inconvenient for quick reference; however, superior photographic results may be achieved as a greater range of specifications are available in this format.

Film for color prints is generally not available for light conditions other than "daylight," so that it can only be used for best results with a daylight flash in actual daylight or with filter accessories in artificial light.

Color prints can be made from transparencies (slides) at any professional photographic laboratory. Of course if you own or have a friend who owns a photo scanner, color prints can be made using a PC.

If you are restricted to a compact camera with no capacity to cope with different light types, and you only have daylight film, it is still possible to cope with nondaylight light. Readily available at most professional camera stores are sheets or rolls of different-colored filter material. By placing the correct color over the nondaylight light (make sure the material is nonflammable) you can alter it to daylight.

Use tungsten film for halogen lights.

Use daylight film for regular camera flashlights.

Use 400 ISO speed (or higher) film for low-light situations.

Use 64 ISO (or lower) film very close-up work. These are the finest-grain films and will give spectacularly clear results.

Halogen Lights

Many portable reading lights and torchères for the home are halogen lights. They use tungsten as the lighting element. Tungsten emits a very bright blue/white light that is quite different from daylight, which is more naturally red. If you use a "daylight" film in your camera, and you light the carving with halogen lighting, the picture will turn out with a red hue, because the film will "see" the light as red. You will need to use a blue filter to counteract this **(11-10)**.

There are many different blue filters; your camera dealer should be able to advise you which is the correct one for your needs. Compact "point-and-shoot" cameras often are not able to accommodate adding filters, so this needs to be taken into consideration if you are considering purchasing one.

11-10 This photograph was taken using daylight film and a tungsten halogen light. A blue filter is needed to counteract red hue produced by the film.

Fluorescent Lights

Fluorescent lights (sometimes also called "neon") are specially made for environments that need low-cost diffused lighting, such as offices and hospitals or other institutions. These kinds of lights are not really satisfactory for photography at all, especially because they do create sufficiently distinct shadows. They also cast a blue hue over your work; using a "daylight" film with fluorescent ighting can be seen in **11-11** and compared to **11-12**, where proper color temperature lighting is used. It must be noted that fluorescent lights are also manufactured in "daylight" varieties, so before you use a color correcting filter, check the labeling (normally printed on the tube) to see which kind it is.

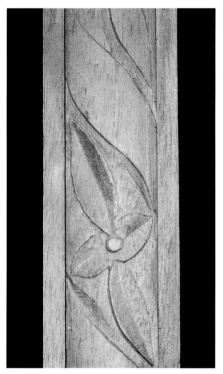

11-11 Neon lights are generally not satisfactory for either carving or photography mainly because they do not create adequate, if any, shadow. It is important to check whether they are "daylight" or not. If not, they will emit a bluish hue.

11-12 This is the same ribbon and leaf pattern as in 11-11 but this time lit with shadow-forming light of a proper color temperature for the film.

Storing Photographs

As most of us with a collection of family snapshots will know, photographs very easily get "out of control," and difficult to find. Digital photography has its own problems because of the large size of the digital files, changing versions of software, and the need to keep a paper reference as well.

Do label each photo print or transparency of a carving or a subject so you can easily identify it years down the track—there is nothing worse than trying to rely on memory. Record what it is, where it was taken, and when. It is possible you might want to go back and take another look at the original sometime in the future.

Store your conventional photographs so they will not easily be damaged. Moisture is a major problem, particularly for prints. The paper they are printed on may attract moisture over a long period so that they may become stuck together. Place some silica gel crystals in the box or drawer where you keep them.

POSITIONING LIGHT SOURCES

As we saw in **11-2** through **11-7**, lighting from different directions creates various effects on shadows. The creation of shadows relies not only on the direction but also the intensity and kind of light relative to the detail on the object as discussed under "Using Different Kinds of Light." For photography and carving alike, it is important to experiment with both so that you can develop the combination that produces the best results for your objectives.

The effects of lighting from different directions on the same subject can be seen by first looking at the opening photograph of this chapter, which shows the shadow effect with lighting from the right. Then look at **11-13** through **11-16**, which show the same object from the left side, straight on, and from above and below. The distance of the light from the subject and the angle of it will impact the length and intensity of the shadow. The only way to work out the best lighting arrangements for your carvings is to experiment. Try lighting directions without taking any photographs, and

Photographing Drawings

Photographing drawings (ink or pencil on white paper) requires special care, otherwise your photograph will come out blank, as a result of gross overexposure. To photograph correctly, your camera will need to have manual settings capability for aperture and shutter speed, or be able to hold an automatic exposure setting using what is known as a photo gray card.

The trap with photographing a drawing on white paper is that the camera normally takes its exposure reading from an area representing a significant proportion of the total area. Unfortunately the major area of the paper is white, not black or whatever color the ink is; the exposure reading will therefore be for a mostly white space. The camera will choose aperture and shutter settings that will be suitable for a white object, and the black lines will barely be visible in the resulting photograph.

The exposure settings need to be adjusted for a darker color than white for the lines to be visible. For this reason we use a "gray card" that represents an averaging of the black ink and white paper. A 17-percent gray color is often used. It is a light gray; if you can't buy a sheet from a camera store, use the inside of a breakfast cereal box, and you will probably get away with it!

Take your exposure against the gray and not the drawing; hold it (or reset your camera accordingly), and the black lines of the drawing should be clearly visible in the photograph when it is processed.

The lighting is important, too. Of course, make sure you have the right film in the camera for the light you are using, but also make sure you have the lights in the right place.

Any artificial light should be directly in front of the drawing (pointing at the same angle as the camera), or if there is more than one light, they must illuminate the drawing evenly, otherwise one side of the drawing will be brighter than the other.

Sometimes, it is possible for the light to shine right through the paper, illuminating a drawing on the other side to cause a double image in the photograph. If this is the case, and you cannot remove the other drawing, it will be necessary to lower the intensity of the light. Make sure the camera lens is at right angles to the entire surface of the drawing, otherwise there will be distortion of the drawing, making it difficult to accurately assess shape and proportion.

then take some from a selection of directions to ensure getting the best results. Keep in mind, you may not get another chance to take any other photographs.

For many reading lights, the replaceable bulbs are available in different beam widths. For photography, a wider beam of light is ideal for casting a broad general light, and a narrower beam of light is ideal for highlighting the subject matter. A combination like this helps remove extraneous background shadows and allows the features of the subject to be clearly seen.

11-13 Shadow effect with lighting from the left.

11-15 Shadow effect with lighting from above.

11-14 Front lighting: Before pressing the shutter button, double-check that you are getting the details you really want. Front lighting shows minimal detail.

11-16 Shadow effect with lighting from below.

Photographing Different Views of the Same Subject

When photographing different views of the same subject, remember to take each of the photographs from exactly the same distance. When we use the shots as reference, it is very difficult to use them comparatively unless they are all of the same scale. Always be sure to record the actual size of the subject. This will enable some scaling to be done at another time, even if the subject is not the same size in all the photos.

A simple solution is to place the subject on a swivel chair, and progressively photograph. It may be necessary to alter the position of the lights, or to take different series of photos each lit differently to create different shadows to reveal different features.

Chapter Twelve

ANATOMICALLY SPEAKING
Details of Anatomy for Artists

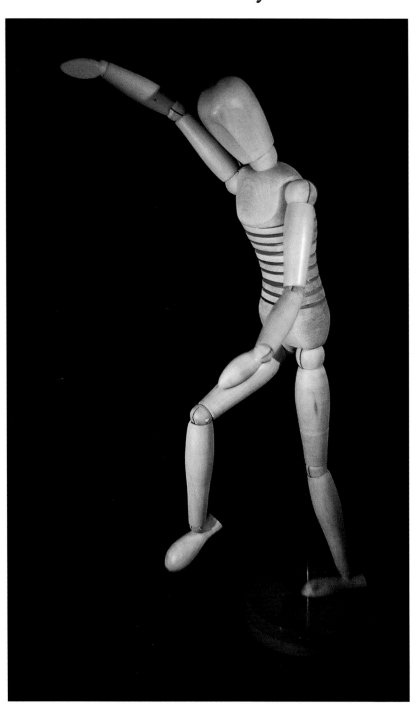

We need to take a look at some things about anatomy in general before we can get to carving forms from living creatures, much less humans. These things will affect how we look at animals, including birds and humans. And that is the key—"how we look at things" is the most important aspect of successfully creating our images of birds and other animals (especially humans!). Then we will be ready for Chapter 13, "Let's Face It," where we will look at some of the ins and outs of carving the human face.

LEARNING HOW TO LOOK AT THINGS

Just as tool technique and timber knowledge need to be learned, so we need to learn the technique for "looking at things" so we see what we really need to see. So far, we have carved likenesses that are not specifically detailed. *Abstract* or *general* shape is a good way to describe what we have done. Previously in this book we have also talked about the art of *observation* being an important part of our new skills bank. In this chapter we will review what we have covered so far, and add the final dimension of observation technique to complete our learning process. Then, all we need to do is practice it!

Keeping an Open, Inquiring Mind

Now is a really good time to turn back and reread the Preface, especially if you haven't already done so. If you have completed just a few of the projects we have described, or substituted some of your own more preferred ones, you will be fairly happy with your progress in the "I can't do that" stakes. In the part of the Preface about "Some things it is helpful to have" we talked about an inquiring mind. This is the very part of our skills bank we need to really nurture now. After you have read this chapter, you will never look at anything the same way again!

Looking Is Different from Observing

For many of us, looking at our own face in the mirror is something that is a necessity rather than something we particularly like doing. We might be self-conscious or embarrassed or whatever. Somehow, though,

12-1 This simple line drawing is done from memory as to what the author thinks his left thumb looks like. Now check 12-2.

Observing Details

The mind tends to register general shapes of birds and other animals and other objects, locking away a general record of what a horse looks like, or what the hand looks like, or what an eagle looks like, in a general sense only. What the mind doesn't automatically do is record the detail of what those things look like. Unless we intentionally focus the mind to do otherwise, the memory we retain consists only of recognizable generalized images of shapes that we can recall and compare with the shapes of new animals or birds we might see.

Don't be at all concerned by this, because until we need to reproduce the specific image of a bird or animal, we have no use for the knowledge. However, as a result of not needing to retain detail, we have not trained our brains to even look for it in the first place; that is what we are about in this chapter.

looking at our hand or foot or knee or fingernail is not such an issue. Nor is looking at someone else's face such an issue; nor is looking at a bird or other animal. In fact, we mostly tend to quite like looking at birds and other animals. So, what we will do is focus only on those anatomical things we like to look at and completely ignore those we don't.

Starting to Observe

First, choose a simple part of your body you look at every day of your life. Don't choose a part of your face, it's too complicated. Choose something simple–your left thumbnail will do. *Don't look at it now; however, pick up your pencil and try to draw it from memory.* Just a simple line drawing is perfect (**12-1**). Does your drawing look something like this? It could be any thumb or finger for that matter, but it is a recognizable basic shape. The trouble is it really doesn't tell you very much at all.

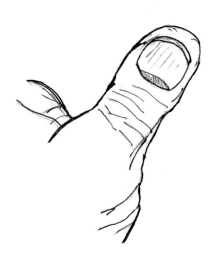

12-2 *This illustration is clearly a left thumb. It is too short for a finger and the fleshy part to the left places it as the thumb of the left hand. Take a look at your left thumb and you can only agree! It certainly is a thumb, and it can't be the right one.*

12-3 *This sketch of a round bird's eye is almost a meaningless circular object. Yet it is also what most bird's eyes look like. See 12-4.*

Look now at **12-2**. This is a quick sketch of what the author's left thumb really looks like. There is no comparison between **12-1** and **12-2**.

Now, all we have done in this simple comparison is compare reality to memory. We took a closer look, studied what we were looking at, and recorded it accordingly. We increased our observation of the actual object and left no doubt as to what our observations told us.

Paying Attention to Context

Now, let's take a look at another example, where *context* makes all the difference to generalized shape. *Context* is a most important part of the observation process. Very often, a shape is meaningless, unless it is set within a context. It's like the previous thumbnail exercise—until the fleshy part of the hand is drawn in, the thumb sketch could be left hand or right hand. Now, look at **12-3**. Here, we have a bird's eye. Most of them are round, or pretty much so anyway. But it is what we put around the eye that distinguishes it from any other eye.

The same round nothing is placed in the context of a particular subject in **12-4**, and we have the makings of an eagle. There is, on the surface, nothing outstanding about this demonstration, except for one thing: that is that unless we view and/or record our specific observations within the context of a particular subject, they are most likely going to be meaningless to us and very forgettable.

12-4 *The same round eye from 12-3 that could belong to any bird is placed within the context of a particular subject, and its meaning is transformed.*

So, now we have the two most important ingredients that will ensure we significantly alter our observation skills and, therefore, the reality of the carvings we create. First, is the specific detail itself, and second is the context in which it exists: *detail* within a given *context*.

In effect, what we are doing is reorganizing the way we think. Instead of remembering a generalization, we are starting to observe and record reality. It is a discipline, but an easy and fun one to get used to. Next time you look at a bird, look at its eye not from the point of view of what does its eye look like, but what does its eye look like in relation to the rest of its head? Does it have an "eyebrow" like an eagle? Is it close to the top of its head or further down its face? Is it in the center of the side of its face or more toward the beak? *You will never look at a bird the same way again!*

LEARNING TO OBSERVE THE HUMAN FACE

Now, let's come back to the human face. If you don't like looking at your own, ask a friend to sit for you. We will focus our attention on the friend's right eye, the one on our left.

Once again, it is vital we look at the *detail* of the eye within its *context* on the face. That is, the eyelid, the cheek, the nose, and the eyebrow—in other words everything that surrounds it. The eyeball itself doesn't really create the character of the eye at all, except for its color, and that is not a variable unless we are planning to color the wood we use for our carving. First, let's take the eyelids. Some questions you can ask yourself as you look at your eye in the mirror, or your friend's eye in front of you, are listed in the accompanying checklist. Each of these questions can, and should, be asked about any eye you wish to reproduce; any one of them represent common features that are overlooked when carving the human eye.

The study of anatomy for reproduction in art should not become a laborious pursuit. Indeed, some of us will have no interest in it at all. However, if you want to reproduce some animals, including people, then it is essential to at least have some fun and give it a go. Use the checklist in the sidebar to the right to help develop your understanding of the detail of your subject's eye. If you go systematically through this checklist, *you will never look at an eye the same way again!*

Checklist—The Detail of an Eye

This checklist is a tool to reinforce the new skill we are developing, which is really the study of *what detail* within *what context*:

What shape is it, and exactly where is it? Are the eyes close together? Is the cheek hollow?

Where is the tip of the nose in relation to the eye and tip of the chin?

Are the corners of the mouth turned up in a smile that extends to the eyes?

Does the top eyelid overlap the bottom at either end? Some eyes have no overlap, others do—mostly on the end nearest the ear.

Is the tissue at the tear duct straight (horizontal) or does it turn down?

How many creases are there on the eyelid? Are there a different number in the top and the bottom?

What is the curvature of the edge of the top and bottom eyelids? Is the bottom eyelid flatter than the top?

How thick is the tissue that forms the eyelid? Is it following the curve of the eyeball on both the inside (where of course it must because it touches it) and the outside?

What is the actual curve of the fleshy part above the eyelid (below the eyebrow)? How wide is it? On some eyes it is pronounced, for others it is narrower.

What is the depth, in relation to the bridge of the nose, of the corner of the eye nearest the nose? It can be quite deep, and it is often made far too shallow, thus not achieving the right roundness of the eye.

What is the position of the other corner of the eye? How far back toward the ear is it? If it is not placed in the right spot, the eye will not be the correct roundness.

USING MEASUREMENTS FOR SCULPTURE

Measurements can establish the relationships that distinquish a subject. In **12-5** we see a roadmap of measurements taken for the sculpture undertaken in the next chapter, seen completed in **13-35**. At the top of this photograph is the note "33%." This is the scale of the photograph in relation to the actual size of the subject. The distances are measured with a pair of dividers and listed separately on paper for easy reference.

For the animal world, which includes birds, the principles are of course the same and just as important. It is the accurate observation of some key shapes that may have a major impact on the effectiveness of the finished work. The shape of the beak and/or tail may be the most important feature that distinguishes one species from another. The size and shape of the elephant's ear will determine whether it is from India or Africa. If the species is important to the work, then the anatomy of the species should be examined.

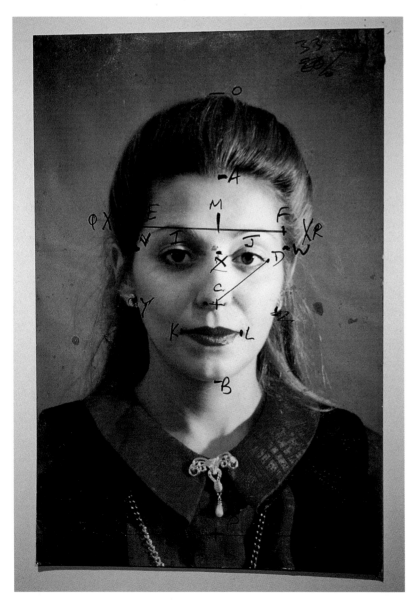

12-5 This is the actual workshop diagram of basic measurements for the carving in the next chapter, shown in 13-35, complete with blobs of modeling wax. The measurements map out the relationships among the key focal points of the face. It is these relationships that help make the face what it is, so it is very important to get them right.

12-6 Plastic small-scale replicas of skeletons are very useful tools for helping to work out concepts for carvings.

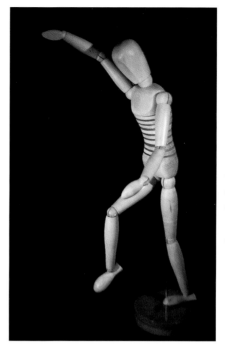

12-7 Another useful aid is a moveable wooden mannequin. Use one together with a skeleton to help make wax models and to assist in the setting up of real-people poses for photography.

ARTISTS' AIDS WE CAN USE FOR CARVING

Sometimes, if we are trying to create a carving of a person in a particular pose, it is a bit difficult for us to develop the concept and then execute it without the help of a mannequin. We may still take photographs of an actual person modeling for the final pose, but our initial thinking needs a bit of help. Available from art supply retailers are a variety of different mannequins and skeletons made just for this purpose. Once again, the relationship between the different parts of the body in different poses becomes an important issue for the success of the sculpture, so these kinds of aids can be very useful (**12-6** and **12-7**).

Developing Your Eye—Some Easy Things You Can Do for Practice

Next time you are sitting in the bus or train, instead of staring idly out the window or immersing yourself in the morning paper, take a look at some of the faces around you. You'll probably be caught staring at someone, so be careful! They mightn't believe you are studying sculpture!

Check the shape of the nose and the corners of the mouth. How close are the eyes to one another? What is the length of the ear in relation to the length of the nose? It's probably about the same. Are the corners of the mouth almost directly below the pupils of the eye? *You'll never look at a face the same way again.*

If you are standing at the bus stop, take a look at how the other people are standing. Is their weight on one foot or equally on both? Are they slouching over? Are both shoulders the same height? If a hand is hanging by the side, where does it come to in relation to the waist? Are the fingers straight or are they slightly bent? *You'll never look at anyone the same way again!*

DETAILS THAT LOOK NATURAL

If you have ever looked at a sculpture or carving and thought "It doesn't look natural," chances are that the reason for this is that the detail of the positioning of the anatomy was incorrect. It is very easy to not get things quite right or make a mistake, so some care needs to be taken. Here is a simple exercise you can do for yourself to prove the point, using just your hand and your carving mallet:

Hold you hand out in front of you as though you were holding your mallet, with the palm of your hand facing you (**12-8**, **12-9**, and **12-10**).

If you were to carve the fingers as they are in **12-10** as opposed to **12-8**, you would have got the naturalness of the anatomy quite wrong, and your work would look contrived or stiff. This is a common fault in many works—all the elements are there, but they are not how the body is in an unstressed (meaning doing nothing) state.

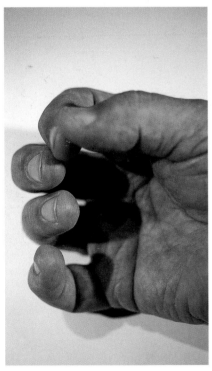

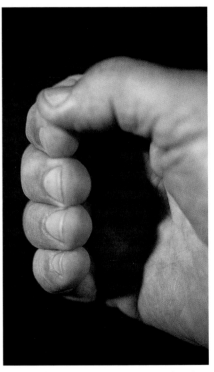

12-8 This is a right hand posing as though it were holding on to the handle of a carving mallet, the handle of which would be in the palm and going between the index finger and thumb. Take special note of the position of the four fingers and the angle of each in relation to one another. This is a natural pose with no stress or tension in any of the fingers. Now, compare the position of the fingers to the same fingers in 12-9.

12-9 The same hand as in 12-8 is now gripping a mallet. Not with a stranglehold, but just in a normal manner. Now, look at 12-10.

12-10 Slide the mallet out, keeping the fingers in the mallet-holding position. Now, compare the positions of the fingers to those in 12-8. Without the mallet, the fingers in this illustration look unnatural. The context of the mallet has been removed, but the fingers remain in "mallet mode," so to speak.

Many people have a tendency, when they put a hand out in front of them to look at, to stiffen the hand and spread the fingers. It is a quite unnatural pose, and is shown in **12-11**. In the same photograph is the right hand in a natural state. There is a significant difference between the two, the right hand being definitely more "natural." Children tend to draw or model the hand as it is in the left hand of **12-11**.

If you would ever like to make a likeness of yourself, you could start with a detailed part of your body. You might find inspiration in **12-12** from one student who created a personally meaningful portrait, in part.

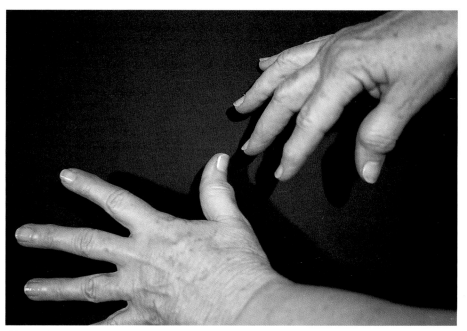

12-11 With this exaggerated example, the stiff hand is very childlike, and the relaxed hand more obviously natural. The anatomy is all there, but it is not in the right place for a natural look.

12-12 A ballet student created a likeness of her own leg. A self-portrait with a difference!

Chapter Thirteen

LET'S FACE IT!
Getting Started Carving Human Sculpture

Most of us at some time or another would like to have a go at carving a human face. There is a real emotional appeal about making a bust of a spouse, friend, or famous person. It is an admirable ambition, and the work can offer some very pleasing results, of which you will be proud. There are some very important aspects to creating any anatomical part, whether human or animal. This chapter is based on the assumption that you would like to carve something that reflects as reasonably as possible a person you know.

Before starting out, it is important to know that the realistic carving of the human form is demanding on both observation skills and time. This is not to suggest in the slightest that you should steer away from your ambition, but it is best to know the challenges up front rather than start out and then become frustrated. Having said that, it is also worth knowing that the successful completion of a bust is an inspiring experience never forgotten.

SETTING UP TO START YOUR PROJECT

Unless you already have photographs or drawings of your subject, the first step, after choosing a subject, is to establish this reference material. Photographs are easiest (**13-1**). If you are unsure of your photography, take the time now to read through Chapter 11 again on photography for woodcarvers.

*13-1 This is the subject for the bust in **13-35**, the same photograph as in **12-5**, but before the series of measurements discussed in Chapter 12 have been added.*

Choosing a Subject

First, the subject. If the person is still alive or is ever likely to know you are making or have made a bust of them, it is best to let them know from the beginning; if there are any objections, then perhaps a rethink of the project may be necessary. If you are happy with the responses, then all is well! Some people have a fear or embarrassment about their image being seen, such as in a photograph, so a painting or a sculpture of them is also often a problem for them. This is best respected, especially as you might want the person to sit for reference photography and also to sit for you during the creation of the work.

A happy subject is a lot better than an uncomfortable one! And there is certainly no point in doing something that will not be a happy experience throughout.

The importance of ensuring the subject agrees with the project and, just as important, the expression/style you want to use, cannot be overstated. If there is not acceptance and agreement between you and the subject, not only will the subject be unhappy, but you will be very disappointed in the nonacceptance of all your good work.

Making Reference Photos of Your Subject

The lighting you use for the photographs is important. It is essential to capture as much detail of contours, lines, and shapes as possible; cross lighting is mostly best for this. Set the subject under an overhead light, and use some reading lights to achieve cross lighting. If this is inconvenient, do the photography outside in the early morning or late afternoon when the shadows are longest; excellent results should be achieved.

Take photographs from different views at regularly indexed intervals all around the person's head. Make sure they are all taken from the same distance. One easy way is to set up your camera on a tripod, sit the

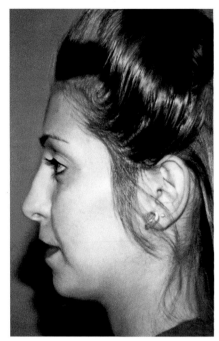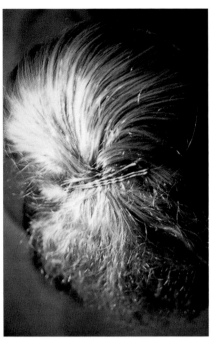

13-2, 13-3, 13-4 These examples are some of the photographs used to make the bust in 13-35. The lighting is severe in some of them to create deep shadow highlights so the real shapes can be easily seen.

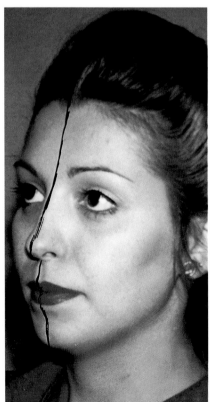

13-5 This is another example used to make the finished bust in 13-35. Note the centerline down the middle of the face to assist in measuring and placing of detail.

13-6. A closeup of facial features. Notice the distortion from orthodontic braces around the subject's lower lip. Braces were also installed behind the upper teeth; allowance was made in the final carving for the altered shape of the facial features once the braces were removed.

person on a swivel office chair, turn him or her around say at one-eighth (of a circle) intervals, adjusting the lighting to highlight the details you want to capture, and taking each photograph accordingly (**13-2, 13-3, 13-4**). Marking on the photographs, as we saw in the previous chapter in **12-5** can be helpful, even when it is as simple as drawing in a centerline (**13-5**).

Take some shots as close as your lens will allow you to focus for specific parts such as ears, nose, mouth, and eyes (**13-6, 13-7**). Also take one looking straight down on the subject's head and another looking up from under the chin.

You will soon understand why some people do not want their likeness being created. Many people remain self-conscious all their lives; it is a normal human characteristic. Close-up photographs of their nose, ears, and so on are the last things they want recorded.

Using Sketches to Study the Subject

Once your photographs are taken, and both yourself and the subject are comfortable with them, move on to the next part of the process: making some sketches.

To follow the learning process in its entirety, do some sketching of the head particularly observing and high-lighting various bone and muscle features that you are able to discern from the photographs you have taken.

The easiest way to do these drawings is to wrap some tracing paper around the print and draw on it with a pencil. The muscle features shown in **13-8** highlight the high roundness of the eye cavity, the prominence of the cheek, and the size of the mouth relative to other features. There is a broad bridge to the nose and a high, wide forehead.

If you look at the two eye formations, you will see that they are not the same shape. The muscles surrounding the right eye (on the left-hand side of the photo facing you) cover a greater (wider) area than those of the left eye (on the right of the photo). If you go back and look at the photo in **13-1**, you will notice that the eye on the left of the photo is larger and rounder than the other eye; this is a most important feature of this face. It is not symmetrical at all. Most faces aren't. Let us continue to draw in a "guesstimate" of the skull shape. The hair on top of the head is about an inch thick, so we can reasonably assume where the top of the skull will be.

13-7 *Another closeup used to make the bust in 13-35.*

13-8 *Notice the eye-muscle areas are different in size and shape, as are the sides of the face. Do the drawings on tracing paper folded over the color print.*

To assist you in this process, it is wise to purchase from an art bookstore or borrow from your local library an "anatomy for artists" handbook. One of these publications will show you many skeletal and muscle formations which all help to give you an understanding of how the human body is put together. This understanding makes it a lot easier to know what to look for on your "observation trail," and therefore you end up with a much better job.

A workshop sketch is shown in **13-9**. At the top right corner is a measurement, "X 3.05." This is the scale of the person's actual head to the size of the print of the photograph. Make a note like this on your drawings. Then when you take a measurement from the photograph you can convert to the carving dimensions with your calculator by multiplying by the scale factor and then multiplying that by the percent for your wax or wood model (e.g., full size = 100%, ⅔ = 66.6%).

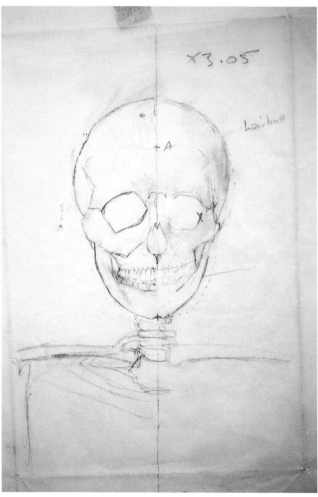

13-9 *Here, the centerline (which really isn't in the center because it is drawn through the center of the nose on the asymmetrical face) is the tool that causes the immediate observation of the difference in the size of the two sides of the head. Yet, when you look at **13-1**, everything looks perfectly normal—because it is perfectly normal for everything to be asymmetrical.*

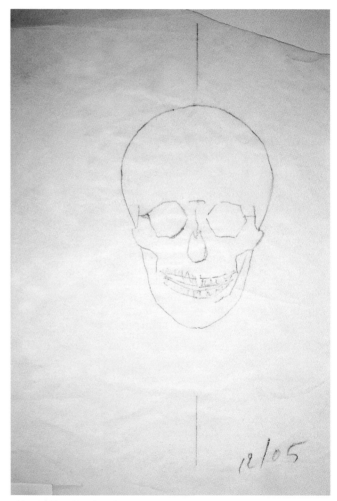

13-10 *This is what happens when the left side of the face (the right-hand side in illustration **13-9**) is duplicated for the opposite side. The head is symmetrical, but is thin compared to the actual person.*

You will see immediately that the head structure is quite asymmetrical. Drawing a line perpendicularly through the center of the nose highlights this. Now look at **13-10** and **13-11**. They are drawings where each side is mirrored on the other. Notice one is a very *thin* head, and the other is a very *wide* head? This is what happens if you make the skull symmetrical—depending on which half you want to duplicate! Had the wax or wood sculptures been made based on either

half, mirrored to form the full head, the result would have been quite wrong, and indeed rather ugly. This asymmetry of natural form is a critical observation. If you don't apply it, you run the very great risk of producing some very unrealistic-looking work. Your left hand isn't necessarily the same as your right, or your feet the same—or your ears!

When you have a go at doing these elementary sketches, you will begin to realize the absolute importance of carefully studying the subject. You should do this as objectively as possible, and take as much time as necessary to fully understand and interpret what you are looking at. Don't let your "assumed" knowledge of what the person looks like get in the way, because it will probably be incorrect.

Some additional drawing you could do is to practice on the shapes of the parts of the head. The eyes are very important, so this is a good place to start. The practice sketch of an eye form, seen in **13-12**, was used to develop the carving in **13-35**. Do as many of these as you think necessary—none are wasted and each will be a little different from the previous one.

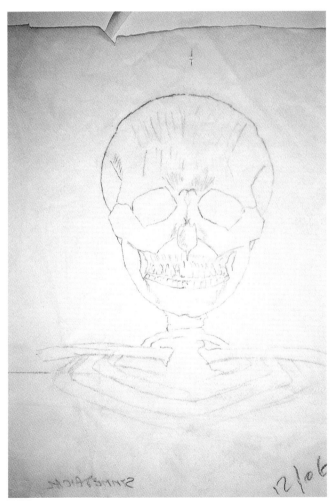

13-11 This is what happens when the right side of the face (the left-hand side in illustration 13-9) is used to duplicate the whole head, and the result is an astonishingly wide extraterrestrial look!

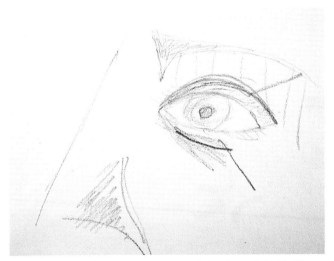

13-12 This is an early concept sketch for the eye in 13-29. In your sketchbook, your drawings are private; no one need ever see them. Therefore there is no need whatsoever to be concerned, be embarrassed, or feel you are a "failure" with your sketches. These sketches are part of your study and learning curve. They are your working out of what goes where and how; they are not art pieces for a gallery for the whole world to see.

Do sketches for at least for the ears and the mouth. There are no specific common faults that should be noted; however, most often not enough time is allocated for studying the subject and getting at least the outlines of the face parts drawn reasonably to scale. So put in the time, in a relaxing and comfortable environment, and you will be amazed at how you perform!

It may help you to do studies of your subject if you become familiar with some of the details discussed in the sidebar below that can make a big difference in how well the carving represents the human face and head. Knowing what to watch out for will help you hone your observation skills.

MAKING A MODEL OF WHAT YOU WANT TO CARVE

If you would like to make a model, or partial model, of your proposed carving, you will significantly extend your learning curve. The advantage of taking this intermediate step is that you will learn the true placement or positioning of the various parts and features of the face, and you can practice on the shapes before cutting them into your wood.

You will be *building up* with your modeling medium rather than carving down in your wood. You can easily experiment and replace on your model those parts

Details to Watch Out for When Making a Bust

The depth of the corner of the eye nearest the nose is often too shallow.

Make sure the eyeballs are round. Often we don't make the corners deep enough, causing them to be too flat. One easy way to get it right is to dig an eye socket, place in it a ball of wax for the eye, and then make and place the eyelids over it.

The shape of the edges of the eyelids is often too flat, and the overlap of top and bottom at the corners is wrong. We are all a bit different; sometimes there is no overlap at all.

The shape of the lips can be deceptive. Start by placing the outline of the lips—the edge that lipstick would fill—in position, and mold inward from there.

Make sure the centerline, the eye line, and mouth line are at right angles to one another.

The facial expression can change markedly by altering the shape of the mouth. First, make sure it is not flat but round (from left to right), following the shape of the cheeks. Then, the line at the junction of the lips can be put in place. Make sure this is deep enough, creating the room to make the curve of the roundness of the lips themselves.

The shape of the forehead is often too flat. The cranium is quite round. Cut out a forehead template from some breakfast cereal box cardboard. Guess the shape to begin with; then test it on the real person. Keep cutting until you get it right! Do the same for the area across the end of the nose and the profile from the hairline to the chin.

The hairline is often too low. It is best to make the head shape without any hair to start with, adding it later. This way, you are more likely to observe exactly where it goes.

The shape of the cheeks is vital to the overall appearance. The whole cheek area is a major part of the face; it is often also too flat. Some cheeks are very prominent, some the opposite. But what ever you do, if you don't get them right, you will be making an error that will influence everything else you do on the face.

13-13 *Modeling tools like these can be used for wax, plaster, plasticine, and clay. Make your own wooden knives and spatulas to any special shape you need, and put to use some of those small workshop scraps.*

that you don't like, whereas with wood, once it is cut off, there isn't a great deal you can do about it if it is wrong.

There is no need to create the bust in its entirety, so the task need not be too daunting.

Choose from your local art supply shop a modeling medium that is convenient to use and that will last without the need for drying out or firing, as is the case for most clay. Modeling media can be a bit messy, so wearing an old shirt is a lot better than wearing the one you wore to the office during the day. You will also need to make or buy some tools for cutting and molding the material you buy. Making them out of scrap wood and wire is fun, although they are so cheap to purchase that the time you use making them might be better spent using them (**13-13** and **13-14**).

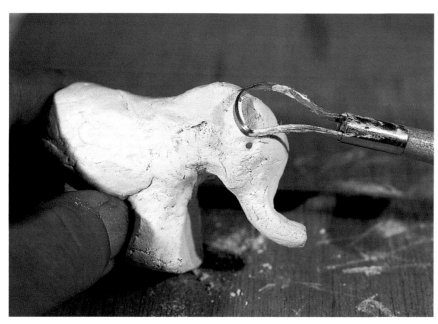

13-14 *The tools don't need to be razor sharp, but they will work a lot better if they are not completely blunt. This will vary a bit depending on which medium you use, so testing is needed to find the optimum. Choose loops made from wire that isn't too thick; wooden knives and spatulas can be sanded sharp.*

Wax is one of the best media, as it is specially manufactured so that it holds its shape once it is at room temperature, but while it is warm it is soft and pliable (**13-15** and **13-16**). Different brands are available from your art supplier, and they also may have a range of different melting points. Seek advice as to the correct one for your model from your retailer. It is easily cut warm or cold. To warm it up, put it in some hot water, or leave it sitting in the sun. In small quantities, it will soften in your hands with body heat. Be sure to follow the manufacturer's instructions (**13-17** and **13-18**).

A firm board is needed on which to create your model. Don't use anything too thin, otherwise it will flex and damage the sculpture. If you make a full-sized wax model, and you make it solid, not only will you use an amazing amount of wax, but also it will be very heavy; you may not be able to lift it. It is better to make it hollow. If you live in a warm climate, it may be that the wax will not stiffen sufficiently to hold its shape if it is hollow, so it will be necessary to fill it so that it will not collapse. You could very easily use crumbled-up paper as a filler (**13-19**).

13-15 This little figure is made from white clay. While readily available, and relatively cheap, clay is not an ideal material for modeling large items such as a full-sized bust. Weight is a major issue; so is cracking and crumbling if the material is not very carefully looked after and in some cases fired. You will be handling the model a lot for measuring and so on, so it is best to use a material that can sustain being touched often and is easy to move.

13-16 Wax is a better material, can withstand handling, and is easy to repair if it is damaged. Always follow the manufacturer's instructions. A smooth, nonlumpy model can be made if the wax is warmed right through evenly and if each small added piece is carefully blended with the original. Larger models can be made hollow and filled with an aerosol-dispensed expanding foam to make them stable and keep them light.

A modern alternative, available from some hardware stores, is an aerosol pack of foam, which is sprayed into the cavity. It expands from liquid to form stiff foam and becomes a very lightweight mass supporting the wax. Use it progressively as you make your model and you have a very stable creation for any situation. It is used for gap-filling insulation and for buoyancy in boat building; so if it is not available at your local hardware store, try a plumbing supplier or a ships chandler.

*13-17 Plasticine can make a good modeling material provided it is firm and not too soft; otherwise it will not hold its shape. This cheerful multicolored model is the plan for the bust in **13-32**. Be careful that the colors don't interfere with your view of the detail. They might make subtle shadows and shapes a little harder to see readily.*

13-18 You will need to experiment with the size of lump of wax you leave in the sun to soften. Softening will depend on the temperature, of course, but also the pieces need to be in a manageable portion for easy use.

13-19 Build up the head piece by piece and create first a hollow skull that can be filled with paper or foam and stabilized. Don't make the wall too thin, as you will want to shape it; however, if you do, and during the shaping process you cut through it, remember it has a stable substance on the inside, and you can easily repair it.

Once you have a starting form, work to define the head and shoulders, adding the decorative features of hair, nose, eyes, and so on. The best methodology is to make a blank head and shoulders to get the basic overall shape how you want it, before adding the "parts" (**13-20**).

Take a look again at the sidebar on page 152 that lists some of the most common things we do incorrectly when we have our first go at a bust. In many instances, the things that are incorrect are subtle. You will discover that "a little bit goes a long way."

Make your learning model the same size as you will your wooden one; it is a simple matter of transferring measurements to it. You can use the real person as a model too. They can sit for you for an hour or two periodically; this will give you good opportunity to get things right. It is important to realize that the modeling material, and the wood itself, will have a significant influence on the look of the work. It is impossible for either to look the same as the real person, because, if nothing else, the textures and colors are quite different; these have an impact on the overall appearance. Wood will always have the qualities of wood, and clay of clay. The hair will be in most cases impossible to recreate accurately, and this also has a strong influence.

Possibly most important of all is the treatment of the eyes. Check your work against the accompanying sidebar on details to watch out for. Experiment on your built-up model. The pupil and the iris are the items in question. Do you carve them in? How do you make the pupil—make a small hole? Do the eyes have to look straight ahead? There are no standard answers, each case having to be dealt with on its merits.

The eyes looked quite "off" when the pupil and iris were added (**13-35**), even in the faintest very subtle way. In this photograph, the eyeball has been lightly colored with shellac, as have the lips; in this way they are distinguished from the rest of the face and give some relief to the mass of wood. Experiment with your model, trying different techniques. If you have any doubts when you are doing the wood version, make a wooden mockup of the eye and try out some of the alternative approaches.

SELECTING WOOD

The choice of wood will of course depend much on what is available in the size you require. Some guidelines that will help you make the right choice are discussed in the sidebars on the next two pages.

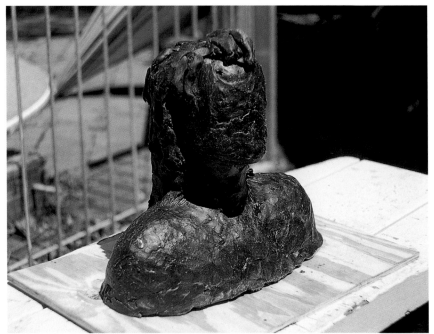

13-20 Before progressing with the detailed modeling of the face and hair, check the stability of the body work by warming it up. This model is sitting in the sun by the swimming pool fence and is quite stable. There is nothing more irritating than coming into the backyard shed in the middle of the afternoon and finding a sagging head on the benchtop!

About Choosing Your Wood: Which Species?

What is available in the size you want will vary considerably from region to region, and country to country. There are some guidelines, however, that will help to make the right choice.

As a part of your decision-making process, it is important to test the wood before you start the carving, and indeed before you purchase it. Most wood dealers will let you push a gouge through the end of a log or block, so make sure you have one with you when you go shopping. So what should you look for? The factors to consider will depend on the style of your sculpture. For example, you could do a chunky, rough-finished caricature, or a smooth, realistic carving, or a stylized image. We will assume you want to do a realistic carving, because the demands on the wood will be the highest:

Choose a straight, finely grained timber. Avoid one that is grainy and splits easily., that is stringy and/or crumbly, or that is spongy.

Test how smooth you can get the surface by using both the gouge and some sandpaper.

Test the ability of the wood to sustain fine edges (for example, around the eyelids and the hair detail) by making some fine grooves very close to one another with a V tool or a skew.

Avoid one that has a lot of figure in it—swirly grain, knots, striped grain, and flecks will interfere with the look of the carving and probably detract from the face detail, unless of course it is a part of the intended design.

There are some unknown challenges that may occur, such as internal checks or knots that will not become evident until you are well advanced with the carving. If you have your eye on a particular species, review some wood texts to see if the species has a common characteristic of internal problems. Some species are prone to these defects; so a little homework is advisable to help avoid a major disappointment. It is difficult to secure a completely blemish-free large block of wood, so there needs to be an acceptance that it is a natural substance, and that, provided the blemish isn't going to ruin the piece, the viewer will accept and ignore any minor markings.

The block of Huon pine from which the bust in **13-35** was carved is shown in **13-21**. This is a reasonably fine-grained species, not too dense, although it can be a little flaky at times. The block was unseasoned at the start of carving, and it was kept sealed on the end grain until completion, by which time it was nearly completely seasoned.

13-21 If possible, avoid a block that includes the pith (at the center) of the log. It may be hollow or very pulpy, or even rotten, and it may badly affect the appearance of the bust. Heartwood is often better quality for carving than sapwood; therefore, for a large carving block, a fairly large tree is needed for supply.

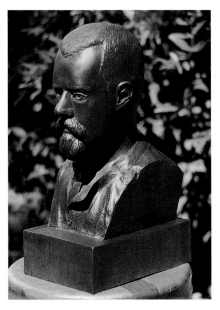

13-22 This bust was carved in rosewood, which seems ideally suited for the formality of this carving. The finish is shellac and wax; the shine is not great but sufficient to make it attractive without its being overdone.

Whtether you start with seasoned or unseasoned wood is a consideration discussed in the sidebar below. The color of the wood also plays an important part in the process of choice. A darker wood **(13-22)** tends to be (but is not necessarily) more formal than a lighter color. Often a darker wood will also offer greater scope for a more visible high polish, if this is the desired effect. Be circumspect about using synthetic finishes such as gloss polyurethane—the end result is mostly gaudy, and very artificial. The softness and mellowness of natural wax offer a very pleasing luster.

CARVING YOUR PROJECT

Tools that you may find useful and/or necessary for carving human sculptural figures are discussed in the sidebar on the opposite page as well as in Appendix 3.

About Choosing Your Wood: Seasoned or Unseasoned

The majority of wood the modern woodcarver will use is kiln-dried as opposed to air-dried, unless it is blocks for sculpture. In these cases it most likely will always be air-dried; this often happens during the carving process. This is simply because the time and energy required for kiln-drying large volumes of large blocks of wood is too great for economic viability.

While kiln-drying does not necessarily affect the ability of the wood to lose or take up moisture with varying humidity conditions, the astute carver may notice in some species a difference during the carving process in the texture of kiln-dried versus air-dried wood. Most might say it is a figment of the imagination; however, there seems to be a marginal tendency for kiln-dried wood to be more brittle, sometimes more crumbly, dry, and generally not as workable as air-dried wood. Chances are that the kiln-dried wood has these characteristics because it is in fact drier than its air-dried counterpart, although if they are both exposed to the same climate for any period of time their moisture content should tend to be equal.

As it is most likely that you will need to air-dry your wood, then here are some tips you can follow:

To help prevent splitting, keep your wood out of direct sunlight and wind, storing it in a cool dry place.

Coat the ends with a sealing compound to help prevent end-grain radial checking (cracking) as the wood dries. The slower it dries, the less the likelihood of degradation.

After each carving session, recoat with end-grain sealer, if necessary.

If a dry spell occurs in the weather (wind may cause a significant drop in humidity level), drape the block being carved with a damp towel. Small amounts of water won't damage the wood, but be careful not to introduce an environment for mold growth. Refer also to Chapter 4, "Natural Wonders."

Tools for Carving Human Sculpture

Refer to Appendix 3 for the gouges you will need for this type of project. The majority of the carving at the early stages is done with a large, reasonably flat gouge; 2 inches (50mm) wide is about the minimum useful size. You will find that a mallet is necessary most of the time with tools this size, as there is a fair amount of power required to push through the wood. Refer to Appendix 3 also for a discusion of mallets.

It will be necessary to have access to a reasonably large band saw to cut the profiles into a block the size you need for a bust; your local professional woodworker will most likely be able to assist you (**13-23**). A range of additional measuring tools you can use are shown in **13-24**.

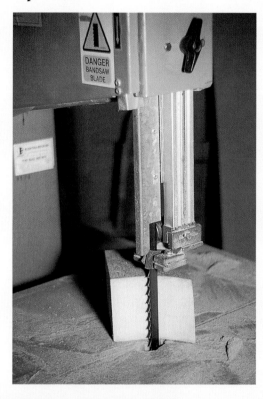

13-23 First, for a work of this size, access to a large band saw is essential, otherwise there will be a lot of labor removing large amounts of waste to get the profile established. A professional woodworker will be able to assist you for a very nominal cost.

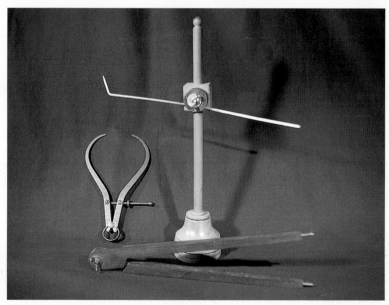

13-24 These measuring instruments will be very useful for making your bust. On the left is an external caliper, which you can use for measuring distances such as the width of the nose, and then marking it off on your wood for carving. In the center is a scribing block, which you can use for transferring heights from a wax model to your wood. In the foreground is a compass or divider, used also for transferring and marking out distances.

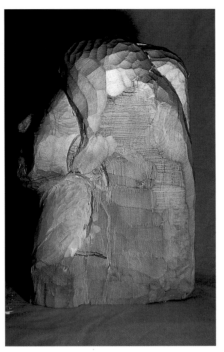

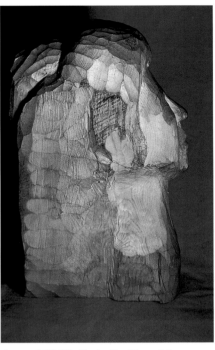

13-25 Cut in the positioning for the eyes, and expose the nose, cheeks, and mouth. Constant measuring with dividers and using a scribing block are not essential but they do save a lot of fiddly measuring.

13-26 and 13-27 These are the left and right views of 13-25. Do both sides at the same time. It is much easier if you do this rather than one side at a time. Make sure, however, that you don't introduce symmetry that isn't there.

13-28 It is also important to work around the sculpture all the time. Take the phrase "carving in the round" literally. Working the sculpture all over helps ensure that you don't introduce a lopsided or otherwise out-of-proportion look.

Copying from Your Model to the Woodcarving

Keep in mind as you begin carving the wood that you want to work around the sculpture all of the time, maintaining a balanced level of progress. Be careful as you work around the figure that you don't introduce any unintended symmetry. The early stages for the carving in **13-35** are shown in **13-25** through **13-28**.

One of the most time-consuming things to try to do is to copy someone else's work. It is one thing to have to work out what to do, but to add to the task by trying to do it in a very particular way is doubly time consuming. When you copy from your model, however, you have the advantage that it was your own work in the first place (**13-28**). The copying process becomes not one of copying for the sake of copying but one of seeing what you did and reproducing it with the intent of changing it for the better.

One way to take measurements for transfer to the block is toe rig up a plumb bob to measure the vertical and the scribing block to measure the horizontal, as shown for another model in **13-29**. Using templates made from your photographs is another easy and effective method for transferring shapes both to model and wood; you can also use this technique to transfer shapes from model to wood (**13-30** and **13-31**).

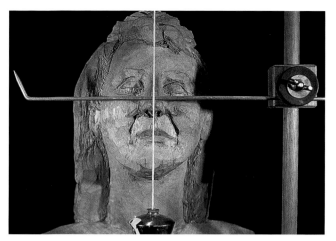

13-29 In the sidebar checklist headed "Details to Watch Out for When Making a Bust," on page 152, we mentioned keeping things at right angles to one another. In this illustration there is such a great error in the eye line that it is impossible to do any kind of justice to the remainder of the face. It is very important to keep these measurements in check to avoid a lot of wasted hours!

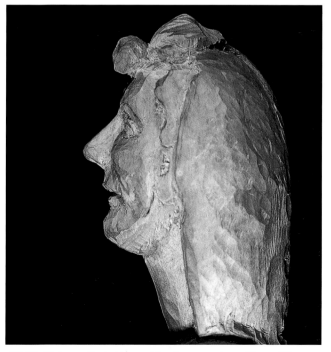

13-31 This profile-in-the-making is a good rendition of the original photograph, with the template from *13-30* being used. If your prints are not the right size, simply scale up the drawing using the grid-line method. Don't use cardboard that is too flimsy, since it will be inaccurate and awkward to use.

13-30 Using templates is an important and easy way to keep the development of profiles on an even keel. If the print is the same size as the proposed finished work, it is easy to simply cut out the profile and trace it onto some stiff card.

13-32 and 13-33 The wax and wood versions show differences in overall appearance and mood. If you are unsure as to the final expression you would like to achieve, modifying the wax version is fast and easy. Experiment as much as you like, before committing it to wood.

FINDING YOUR OWN CREATIVE PROCESS

At the beginning of this book, toward the end of the Preface, we said that "being creative is the act of expressing emotion." This can be done in many different ways. Singing a song. Writing a book. Composing a poem. They are all expressions of emotion; so is woodcarving. If you have never effectively expressed your emotions in art, which may be because you have never had the opportunity, or because you never thought you could, or any one of a hundred reasons, which don't really matter, then you have never exposed your true creative ability. It remains latent within you.

13-34 There is always room to alter the expression and even the overall look of your sculpture when you transfer it to wood. In this case the artist wanted a happier expression for "Laughing Boy," which was certainly achieved!

In the following examples, there are some important observations that highlight key attributes of the creative process, especially in the subtle and not-so-subtle differences from model to wood and in the expressions of emotion.

Portraits of Mozart in wax and wood are seen in **13-32** and **13-33**. The darker wood (mahogany with shellac and wax finish) suits the formality and "seriousness" of the piece. As you can clearly see, there are differences between the wax and wood versions—in poise, expression, and overall appearance. Also in the wood version there is a dark stripe that appeared as the carving progressed; this can be seen around the perimeter of the face. It could be argued that it spoils the work, particularly when viewed from the angle in **13-33**. It accentuates the oval appearance of the face. This oval appearance is not so pronounced in the wax version, and, without the interference from any stripe, it is even less so.

Expressions of Emotion

The wooden version and its plasticine model (which we have seen in **13-17**) are shown in **13-34**. While the wooden face is quite clearly modeled on the colored version, it is nevertheless distinctly different. In this case, the artist has taken the elements of the original to create a wooden version that arguably expresses a "funnier" look. The photograph on the opening page of this chapter, page 146, shows this piece between two other carvings started by the same artist. This is an extraordinary example of a competent artist who carved the emotions she felt without even knowing she was doing it. This person had not realized, until she gave permission for these examples to be shown in this book, that for years she had expressed her true emotions through the art she did. She knew what she liked and didn't like, but until now she wasn't aware that her creativity was an expression of her emotion. The unfinished faces (and they probably will remain unfinished) on either side of "Laughing Boy," on page 152, are decidedly unhappy. Miserable even. They are busts in the making of real people; "Laughing Boy" is a made-up fun face.

The carver admitted frequently that she was finding the going very hard with the two "real" people, but that she thoroughly enjoyed the creation of the happy, funny, fictitious face. The face on the right of the woman she abandoned because it "just wasn't happening," and the face on the left took too long for little progress. What this person didn't realize was that she was carving her emotions.

If you go into this person's house, and if you get to know this person, you will find a great and funny sense of humor. Other self-created art she does is cheerful, humorous, and lighthearted—sketches of caricatures and clay models of clowns. Very little if anything she likes is too real; her favorite carving subject is gargoyles. Ugly mythical creatures!

This artist actually finds no pleasure in the carving of realistic things, and, unknown to her, the carving she was finding hard going made her miserable; she carved it into the expressions on the faces of the real people. She unknowingly recreated her feelings about what she was doing in her very work. Carving real people made her unhappy, and that is exactly how she carved them. The two "real" people carvings were attempted about a year apart.

The important message here is that if you don't really like something, and if it doesn't really "turn you on," then don't do it! It will only make you miserable. Don't try to create a bust for the sake of it. Create it because you really want to.

13-35 *The Huon pine and rosewood bust of the international singer Lubika is mounted on a pedestal also of Huon pine.*

THE FINISHED CARVING

Now that you have worked to finish your bust, ensure that the display of your finished carving complements the work and shows it off to best advantage. The finished carving of our subject from **13-1** is shown on its display pedestal in **13-35**.

APPENDIX 1
20 Frequently Asked Questions about Wood

1. Which Is the Best Wood to Use?

This is the most often asked question of all about wood. As we said in the very beginning, any wood can be carved. It is just that some are easier and more appropriate than others for a particular application. The greater the knowledge of available woods, the better equipped is the user for the most appropriate answer. However, as with most things, the "right" choice will be a function of the equilibrium between the key elements in the "which wood?" equation. These elements are the choices of available wood, the carver and his or her current expertise, the tools available to the carver, as well as the design and its end use or application.

A highly skilled carver will be able to carve many species with equal effectiveness, and with few tools generate executions of complex designs. However, there is not much point carving a wood that rots quickly for use as an outside garden sculpture, or one that is really soft for use as an item of everyday furniture. The obvious exclusions often narrow the field quite considerably and very quickly, particularly if the range of available species is not great.

The "best" answer to this question is to research as much as possible the variety of woods that are in fact available; determine their characteristics and apply these to the functional use of the carving. Then balance this information with available tools, design, and expertise. It is the level of expertise that will most likely be the deciding factor in the setting up of the needed equilibrium.

2. Can I Carve This Wood?

You can carve any wood, provided there is equilibrium between the key elements in the "can I carve it?" equation. These elements are the tools available to the carver, the shapes of the bevels on those tools, the expertise of the carver, and the chosen design.

Limitations imposed by the design and the available tools will quickly eliminate many wood options. For example, if there are only very large sculptural tools available, intricate relief carvings will not be possible. The expertise of the carver will naturally increase as a function of practice and experimentation, and this may mean that larger tools can be used for smaller things with greater ease. Once the obvious is eliminated, the field can narrow quickly; the deciding factor will be the preparation of the tools themselves—meaning the shapes of their bevels and the degree of sharpness.

For the majority of woods, tools need no special preparation except to make sure they are as sharp as possible. But for some, it is necessary to alter the curve of the tool's bevel so it can cut effectively. Harder woods may need secondary internal bevels, softer woods longer and thinner bevels, deep curving designs rounder bevels, and shallow designs flatter bevels. See also Appendix 2.

3. Where Can I Get Wood?

In some countries such as on the African continent, wood is a relatively scarce resource. In others such as Australia, wood is so plentiful as to be often disregarded as a valuable asset. One of the great ironies is that those used to scavenging will know almost instinctively where to go to get it, and, for those for whom there is plenty, there is a surprising lack of knowledge as to its whereabouts.

Apart from wood that is available at commercial lumberyards and wood that can be found in its natural environment, there are many perhaps less obvious, but nevertheless very effective, sources of wood for the carver. Demolition sites for old houses, as well as public and commercial buildings, often reveal many treasures of timber in reasonably large cross sections (from roof beams and pillars for example). They will most likely be harder woods, often rich in color and suitable for sculpture. Recycling old tables, desks, and cupboards will uncover excellent wood for panels, boxes, and such.

In many countries, most of the wood that is generated from land clearing for farming or building is destroyed, often by burning. Similarly, the wood from tree pruning and removal from domestic gardens offers a very convenient source of a great variety of species for the carver. Fruit wood is excellent for carving, so local orchards should be on the shopping list.

4. How Long until My Wood Is Dry?

"Wet" or unseasoned wood will ultimately lose water and dry to a level of moisture content so that this is in equilibrium with the surrounding or ambient moisture level of the atmosphere. This moisture level will vary from one geographic location to another, depending on the weather conditions. The time taken for the wood to reach equilibrium with the atmosphere will depend on a variety of factors. These include the initial difference between the two moisture levels, the nature of the cellular structure of the wood, the degree to which the wood is exposed to the atmosphere (for example, leaving the bark on will retard the process), and the prevailing weather.

Unseasoned wood can be carved; often it is easier to carve than when it is dry, because when dry it is often too hard. The denser the species, generally the harder it gets as it dries out. During the carving process, much of the wet wood will be removed and certainly the surface area exposed to the atmosphere will be increased, speeding up the drying rate.

There is no definitive answer to the "how long to dry?" question unless the drying is done artificially in controlled, and previously established, conditions in a drying kiln. There are some "unofficial" rules of thumb, such as for hardwoods it takes a year an inch of diameter in log form for the log to air-dry, but these "rules" are so loose as to have little practical value.

5. How Do I Season My Wood Logs?

For the home carver who has no access to commercial wood-drying facilities, seasoning wood is a relatively easy if time-consuming proposition. There are some basic principles that must be followed; with due diligence the wood should season without many if any problems developing.

Unless the bark is needed, remove it to speed up the process. Use a hatchet or bench axe for this.

Seal the ends of the log with a commercial end-grain sealer, or if none is available, use candle wax or an equivalent. The principal requirement is that the substance must be nonporous. Paint, particularly acrylic, is unsuitable, as it is often porous. It is important to "force" moisture loss from the sides of the log, and not the ends. This helps reduce end-grain checking as the wood's cells will often collapse as the result of too great a rate of moisture loss. Slow drying is better than fast drying.

If storage space is restricted, store the log on its end, remembering to rotate the log end to end at frequent intervals, say every four weeks. This will stop water gathering all at one end. Some species can hold a lot of water during their growing season. Camphor laurel, for example, cut during the growth season, can be so saturated with water that it literally runs out if a log is upended before being sealed.

The end of the log pointing to the ground must be raised from it (sit it on a scrap of dry wood about one inch thick) so that there can be no uptake of mold, moisture, or infection from insect life, and also ventilation can be improved.

Keep your wood out of direct sunlight, wind (which will dehydrate it too quickly), and rain, and do not expose it to significant fluctuations in temperature such as in a shed that gets very hot during the day but very cold at night. Ensure that there is good ventilation all around the log.

6. How Do I Season My Wood Boards?

Boards are seasoned in the same manner as logs, except that it is best to store boards horizontally. This ensures that they are adequately ventilated; they are stacked one on top of the other (to utilize space better), separated from the floor and one another by "stickers." Stickers are scraps of wood cut to the same dimension and laid between boards at intervals—close enough together to ensure the boards do not sag under their own weight. Narrow and thin boards might warp or cup as they dry; to help prevent this, it is a good idea to add some weights (such as house bricks) to the top of the stack.

7. How Can I Stop My Wood from Cracking?

If the above techniques have not prevented the wood from cracking, it is probable that either the measures taken are not being effectively implemented, or the wood is prone to cracking during its drying phase and there is little that can be done in a home environment.

Should cracks or checks appear, review the efficacy of the storage conditions, and if they are considered adequate, some additional "tricks" could be tried:

Fill the cracks with the sealing compound used on the end grain of the board or log. This should stop further rapid moisture loss from the area.

Turn the board or log so the crack is on the bottom where moisture may collect.

Cut off the cracked wood so that it does not create a situation where it takes the remainder of the wood with it. Effectively seal the new end.

8. What Can I Do If My Wood Cracks?

If the wood has cracks that cannot be cut away, there are not a lot of choices in terms of "doing something about them." They can be ignored, and accepted as part of the organic, natural, and imperfect substance wood is. In most cases this is the most philosophical if not also the most practical approach.

It is possible to fill the crack with slivers of the same wood, and in many cases this will effectively hide the crack once they are carved over as though it were solid wood. Synthetic fillers may also hide small cracks. A filler can be homemade from sanding dust and clear drying glue.

Depending on the design, it may be possible to locate it so that the crack is avoided, or marginal modification of the design may achieve the same result.

9. Will This Crack Get Any Worse?

Now this is a million-dollar question! If the wood is seasoned to equilibrium with the ambient atmospheric moisture, and this remains stable, then chances are the wood has stabilized, and there will be no further degradation. If the atmospheric conditions alter, it is possible that further activity may take place.

As a natural substance that is able to take up and release moisture, wood is able to expand and contract, and does, as moisture content varies. The degree of expansion and contraction will depend on the cellular construction of the species; a few days of atmospheric moisture increase or decrease may have no visible impact at all.

If there is any doubt or if there is a potential problem that may arise if the crack does get any worse, the best insurance is to seal the wood so that it cannot release or take up any further moisture.

Some species, such as sassafras, react quickly to increases in moisture content; placing checked timber under a running tap can produce immediate closure of a minor crack. With this in mind, test the species with topical application of water. If it reduces the size of the crack (it may be necessary to leave it for a day or two) it may be that water can be added to the wood to repair it. Then seal it to contain the added moisture to help prevent the return of the crack.

10. Can I Straighten This Warped Wood?

Generally the answer is no. The position is similar to the crack that can't be removed (see Question 7). The wood is warped because the cells that make it up have collapsed, becoming misshapen as they have dried out. Unless these cells can be reshaped to allow the wood to change shape without breaking it, then the warp cannot be removed unless wood is cut away.

Steaming wood is one way to replace moisture, softening the cell walls so they can be forced under pressure of a jig or other device to take on a revised shape. This of course is the principle of steam bending. Larger pieces of timber are steamed with difficulty, as the delivery of the steam to the wood requires adequate steam-generating capability and a steam box large enough to accommodate the wood while the process takes place. Immersion of the wood in water may cause sufficient moisture uptake that will allow the warp to be removed; however, this is mostly ineffective.

An alternative commonly used where the thickness of the timber is sufficient is the planing of the faces of the timber back to a parallel format. The convex and concave surfaces are planed flat and parallel to restore the remainder of the board to a usable condition.

11. What If I Break Something off My Carving?

This is one of the greatest fears of the carver. "I am frightened I'll break something off" is a common catch-phrase. Well, fear not! With modern technology, there are some fabulous glues available. But before that is tried, see if the design can be modified to accommodate the break—in many cases, the removal of the broken area actually improves the look, and certainly may make the carving more practical.

When a break occurs, try to determine why it happened in the first place. Poor technique is not always the reason. It may be that the wood is inappropriate for the design, or vice versa, or it may be that the design has not been thought through adequately, and it is prone to easy breakage. Simple design alterations may resolve the problem.

If none of the above is a desirable alternative, then gluing is the only option. For small breaks, cyanoacrylate (CA or superglue) may be best; for larger repairs, a clear-drying polyvinyl-acetate (PVA) glue may be best.

12. How Do I Stop My Wood from Splitting When I Use the Chisel?

Wood splitting under the chisel is generally a sign of poor tool technique, unless the wood is being cut along the lay of the cells and is a wood that is characteristically stringy. If this is the case, there is little that can be done, except to use great care and patience. Stringy wood is difficult to handle along the grain because the cutting action is such that all it does is dig out bundles of fibers. Unless they are regularly cut off somewhere along their length to allow them to be removed easily, they will always tend to leave a messy appearance. Stringy woods are not favored for relief carving for this reason; they may be more suitable for carving in the round.

If the chisel is pushed through the wood against the grain it will also tend to split and give a broken appearance. If this occurs, reverse the direction of the cut. It is always best to experiment with the cutting direction until the most favorable one is found. Nor should it be assumed that grain direction and cutting receptiveness are constant throughout the same piece of wood. If the

wood continues to be messy when cutting along the grain, the best alternative is to cut across it wherever possible, ensuring only a very sharp tool is used.

13. How Do I Stop the Edges of My Wood from Chipping When I Use the Chisel?

Chipped edges are usually a sign of the wrong wood for the design, cutting in the wrong direction, or cutting with a blunt tool.

Some woods will not easily sustain sharp rises or sharp edges. They tend to crumble if the cross section becomes very small. Brittle woods are certainly likely to behave in this manner.

Ensure the direction of the cut is from the outside to the inside where there is supporting wood to take the pressure of the tool. If chipping still occurs, and the tool is sharp, then the most likely outcome is that there is incompatibility between the wood and the design. Chamfer the edges if the problem continues—this often improves the look of the design as well.

14. What If There Are Knots in My Wood?

If there are no aesthetic reasons to avoid knots, then the only considerations are that the knot may work loose and fall out, or it may cause damage to the tools during the carving process, or it may be so hard it can't be carved effectively.

A knot has its grain flowing at 90 degrees to the grain of the main timber; therefore, its direction of cell shrinkage is different. It may become smaller than the hole in the grain where it is embedded and work loose as the wood dries completely. Knowledge of the species will help in assessing this potential risk.

Because the knot is showing its end grain through the long grain of the main timber, it will cut differently than the long grain, and this may also cause problems with potential tear-out or breakage.

The wood cells in a knot are often denser than the main timber; when dry the knot may cause damage to the cutting edge of the tool. Testing the knot with a chisel before commencing the carving is the only way to assess the likelihood of damage.

15. How Can I Change the Color of My Wood?

Modifying the color of wood is not difficult with the many modern wood stains and chemicals that can be readily purchased.

What is difficult is achieving exactly the color you want. It is important to realize that with most coloring systems, once they are applied to raw wood they cannot be removed. Even solid-color paint will penetrate the cells to some degree. Thorough sealing of the surface of the wood with a sealer will prevent color absorption. It is important to experiment with surface coloring on offcuts from the same wood stock before applying any stains. If the stain mixture is varied during testing, such as by dilution with a solvent, it is important to write down the mix ratio rather than rely on memory. Once applied to the wood, it cannot be easily altered if it is not the right color. Always be sure to read manufacturer's instructions.

16. Which Way Should the Grain Run?

Grain direction is important for two principal consider-ations: appearance and strength. The stripes in woods, such as in zebrawood, olive, and Douglas fir, can significantly alter the appearance of the finished carving, compared to a plain wood. Careful consider-ation needs to be given to grain-direction decisions in circumstances where woods like these are choices. Sometimes the different colors within the same wood are also of significantly different densities, as in the case of Douglas fir, so extra care needs to be taken during the carving process.

In the case of strength, for example with the legs of animals for carvings in the round, the grain direction is better placed along the length of legs rather than across, particularly for smaller cross sections. See also Chapter 7, "Rounder Rumblings." If there is a tail pointing hor-izontally, it may be better to make this from a separate piece of wood, and glue it into place, than to have a vertical grain direction making it likely to break.

For relief carvings, if it is possible given the amount of wood that is available, it may be preferable to have the grain running in a direction other than vertically or horizontally. Where there is fine foliage moving diago-nally, better results may be achieved for both appear-ance and strength if the pattern is moved around the wood until a generally diagonal grain direction is found.

17. Why Is My Wood Changing Color as I Carve It?

Freshly cut wood will always be a different color from wood that has been exposed to ultraviolet light. Natural sunlight will oxidize the wood; the color will gradually change, becoming darker at first, and then eventually going a silvery gray. There are some wood finishes available commercially that will retard the oxidation process by coating the surface with an ultraviolet-light filter in the same way a personal sunscreen does.

It is important the carver realizes this oxidation process will occur, with some woods very quickly and with other woods more slowly. It is very disappointing to see a beautiful freshly finished carving go a much darker shade if it was unexpected. Outdoor carvings will weather more quickly than indoor, so planning the landscaping around a color of wood is not a particularly successful strategy.

18. Should I Sand My Carving?

There is a myth about the use of sandpaper that sug-gests a professional finish does not include its use. The truth is that if sandpaper is a requisite to achieve the desired effect, then its use is essential. Whatever the case, the user must be aware that sanding of any kind will alter the surface texture; this in turn may alter its color, at least until the effect of ultraviolet light takes hold. Sanding will round off sharp edges, softening crisp detail, unless it is done with great care. An off-the-chisel finish, where sanding is not done, imparts a characteristically "hand-done" feel to the finished piece, and sanding will ultimately remove all traces of this. If there is any doubt, test the effects of sanding on offcuts before applying it to the carving.

19. Can I Glue Pieces to Make a Block?

Often when the size of wood required is simply not available, laminating pieces to form a block is the only practical solution. Gluing pieces together to form a hollow block also reduces weight. Rocking horses are traditionally made hollow to keep them light and from a number of different-sized pieces to reduce waste. When laminating is the option taken, there are some principles to follow that may make the gluing and carving processes easier.

Where possible, make sure the grain direction is uniform throughout the glued-up block—this makes the carving process less of a hazard.

Follow the glue manufacturer's instructions. If there is any doubt as to the suitability of the wood for gluing, wash the surfaces with alcohol (methylated spirit) or acetone to remove resins and waxes, and use internal pegs or gluing dowels to help ensure stability.

Choose glue that will not damage carving tools when it is fully cured.

Avoid glue joins in locations where the design will bring the join to a fine edge; thin cross sections of wood expand and contract readily, leading to the degradation of the glued join. This process is called feathering, in which the join separates into two halves. If a thin join cannot be avoided, a sealer should be used to protect the surfaces from moisture uptake and loss.

Ensure the pieces are well and equally seasoned to avoid glue-line cracks' appearing as a result of uneven shrinkage.

Many timbers will carve in made-up block form so that the grain in each piece melds with the grain in the next piece, making the join invisible. Softer woolly woods do this exceptionally well. The finer the joinery,

the more the likelihood that no join will be seen. Use visually grainy woods, such as mahogany or cedar, to help hide any joins. Try to match color and grain configuration when preparing the blocks before gluing.

20. How Often Should I Refinish My Carving?

First, it is important to put some kind of surface finish on carved wood, to protect it from becoming impregnated with dust. An ultraviolet-light filter may also be used to help stop color change. Whatever finish is finally used, it is important to understand the nature of it—what is likely to happen to it and, therefore, affect over time the appearance of the finished work.

Essentially, there are two kinds of surface finish: those that create a nonporous barrier between the atmosphere and the wood, and those that don't. There are many degrees in between, but they will be skewed in one direction or the other. A porous finish such as furniture wax will tend to absorb into the wood; eventually it will need replacing if placed directly on the surface without a nonporous barrier being applied first. A nonporous barrier will tend to fill the grain; if sufficient finish is applied in the first instance, it will sit on the surface and seal it indefinitely—unless the wood expands and contracts so that the seal is broken. This barrier will stop porous finishes like wax from absorbing into the wood; therefore, they will need replenishing much less frequently.

APPENDIX 2
20 Frequently Asked Questions about Tool Sharpening

1. What Sort of Sharpening Stone Should I Use?

Commonly, a flat bench stone is used for sharpening tools. Unfortunately, for woodcarving tools this is inappropriate. A bench stone is designed for sharpening flat tools such as carpenter's chisels. These are sharpened with a constant bevel angle, by moving the tool back and forth across the surface of the stone resting on a bench.

Woodcarving tools are commonly convex in their cross section, and may have a slight convex curve on their bevel. To sharpen them, it is necessary to use a small slip stone that can be held in the hand in such a position as you can see what you are doing. Hold the slip stone between the thumb and forefinger, and roll it over the surface of the tool. Best control is achieved by moving the stone around the tool, rather than the tool around the stone (**A2-1**).

A2-1 Hold the small slip stone so that you can see what you are doing, and roll the stone around the tool for best control. Rock the tool on its convex curve as you grind the surface. Once a burr is formed on the cutting edge of the tool, stop grinding, and gently remove it with the curved spine of the slip stone. Stropping is the next step in the sharpening process.

2. What Lubricant Should I Use on My Slip Stone?

The lubricant you use is not critical; however, it is important to use one. This is because it helps to stop the stone from becoming clogged by metal filings and it helps to wash the metal filings away from the surface of the stone so that you are not simply grinding metal on metal.

Commonly used lubricants are water, kerosene, mineral oil, and cooking oil. Traditionally, the woodcarver used neat's-foot oil, which is made from animal hoofs and is mostly used as a leather preservative for saddles and the like. Neat's-foot oil does not irritate the skin and doesn't clog the stone quite as much as mineral oil. Neat's-foot oil also has the advantage of tending to float the steel particles away from the cutting edge so that the stone is clear of metal filings in the area being used for sharpening.

3. What Kind of Grinding Wheel Should I Use?

Grinding a tool on a wheel on a bench grinder is necessary only to either reshape the tool after considerable wear or to reshape it after it has been chipped or broken. As it will be necessary to polish your woodcarving tools for maximum performance, the less damage the grinding wheel does the better, so a finer wheel is better than a coarser one. Choose a wheel that has a grit size anywhere between 120 and 150, and that is closely compacted to make a smooth surface. A fine grit size openly bonded together can make a surface that is too rough.

Note that it is the side of the wheel, not the edge (circumference) that is used; so this is the surface that needs to be smooth. See Question 6 below.

An aluminum oxide wheel, which would normally be white or orange, is best for grinding woodcarving tools (**A2-2**).

A2-2 Purchase a bench grinder that is free of vibration from the motor. Sometimes vibration is also the result of a poorly positioned grinding wheel, which may need reseating on the spindle. Make sure that the height of the wheel is convenient for you to use and that the space you are using is not too cramped. Best grinding results are achieved when you are relaxed and comfortable.

4. What Diameter Grinding Wheel Should I Use?

For woodcarving tools, what diameter grinding wheel to use is not particularly important. The only important consideration is that the wheel should be large enough for comfortable use. Generally, a standard 6-inch (150mm) diameter wheel is satisfactory.

It is important to note that the circumference or edge of the wheel facing you is not the surface that is used for grinding a woodcarving tool. If this edge is used, you will transfer the convex curve of the circumference of the wheel to the bevel of the carving tool and make it into a concave curve, called *hollow-grinding*.

Hollow-grinding the bevel is inappropriate for a carving tool, since it will tend to make the tool nose-dive into the wood, rendering the tool unusable. A very slightly convex bevel is best, because this helps the tool exit the timber. The convex curve of the bevel actually pushes the tool out of the wood.

Hollow-grinding is very appropriate, however, for a woodturning gouge that is used for spindle turning on a lathe. As a general rule the wood turner will find that an 8-inch (200mm)-diameter wheel offers the best concave or hollow-ground bevel curve. Be careful if you ask a wood turner to grind your carving tools, because he may instinctively, and unwittingly, hollow-grind them.

5. How Do I Know When to Use a Grinding Wheel?

You will want to use a grinding wheel sparingly, since a wheel will tend to remove a reasonable amount of tool steel in the grinding process. Thus the grinding process atually reduces the usable steel in the tool and therefore shortens its effective life.

If you find that the tool cannot be effectively reshaped using a slip stone, then a grinding wheel will be necessary. By the same token a slip stone is a relatively slow way to reshape a tool; so if there is a major task to be done, and limited time, then a wheel is probably necessary.

Large chips, badly misshapen cutting edges, and bevels that need reshaping are three common situations that require the use of a wheel.

Have a small container of water on hand to dip the tool in to keep it cool. Your should also avoid over-heating the tool (which will destroy its temper or hardness) by using only very light pressure on it against the wheel.

6. Do I Need to Clean My Sharpening Stones?

It is very important to keep grinding wheels and slip stones clean.

For the slip stone, regularly soak it in mineral turpentine and scrub it with household detergent. A clogged stone will not cut metal; and you run the risk of rubbing metal on metal.

A grinding wheel that is clogged with metal filings can be a major hazard for your tools. The small gaps between the grit particles that the wheel is made from will become clogged with metal filings; instead of cutting the tool with the stone, you will once again end up grinding steel on steel, overheating the tool, and potentially destroying it.

A2-3 A flat diamond paddle dresser is the easiest to use for dressing the surface of the grinding wheel. Do not apply too much pressure; rather, allow the diamond dust to do its work without any residual damage to it or the wheel.

Keep the grinding wheel clean by "dressing" it with a diamond tip or a diamond paddle that will grind off the used surface of the wheel and expose a pristine grinding surface. Eventually, of course, the wheel will become worn and need replacing **(A2-3)**.

7. What Is the Correct Bevel Angle for a Carving Tool?

There is no single answer to this question, except to offer a not particularly helpful but nevertheless truthful "whichever angle works best for you."

As with all sharpening practice, the "correct" angle of the bevel is the one that provides the equilibrium among the positions in which your hands are most comfortable working, the density of the wood being carved, and the design depth of the carving.

Your comfort zone for posture will dictate an angle of approach of the tool to the wood. This will vary slightly person to person, as someone with small hands will most likely have a different approach than a person with bigger hands. The angle of the bevel itself

convex bevel

A2-4 Cleaning the bottom of curves (for example, in bowl carving) may require grinding the bevel to a suitable curve and/or using a long bent or a short bent tool and certainly some experimentation with grain direction will be necessary to achieve a clean cut.

will also dictate an angle of approach of the tool to the wood, so your posture needs to be in tune with this (and vice versa), otherwise the bevel of the tool will not allow for efficient cutting of the wood.

The denser the wood (i.e., the harder it is), the more likely a long, fine bevel will fracture or break off, because it will be too thin, and therefore too weak. On the other hand, a longer, thinner bevel is more suitable for softer wood, which will not cause it to break so easily. The optimal bevel for flat-surface carving is the one that gives the thinnest cross section of the tool, because it means there is less bulk of tool steel, and therefore less resistance to its being pushed through the wood.

As the depth of the carving increases, from a flat surface to a deep bowl, for example, a greater convex curve will be of assistance to the cutting action. A convex bevel will cut a concave hole more easily than a flat bevel **(A2-4)**.

8. What Is a Secondary Bevel?

A secondary bevel is a second bevel applied to the tool to make certain cutting situations easier. For woodcarving tools, this second bevel might be applied to the inside of the tool, thus increasing the thickness of the tool steel in its cross section and making the front end of the tool stronger. This might be done in cases where there is a lot of carving to be done in denser wood,

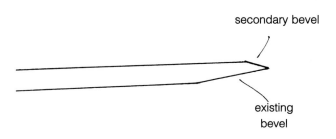

A2-5 *If you are to do a lot of carving in harder wood, place a secondary bevel on the inside of the tool, keeping the angle of approach of the tool constant, while increasing the strength of the steel in the face of the tool.*

rather than making the primary or "normal" bevel of the tool thicker by making it more convex. A more convex bevel will make the approach of the tool to the wood higher and, therefore, harder to push through the wood, because the resistance of it will be greater and more energy will be required.

The primary bevel angle can be maintained by placing the second bevel on the inside of the tool (**A2-5**). It will be necessary to use a slip stone like that shown in **A2-6** to place the secondary bevel in position.

A2-6 *A cylindrical slip stone is needed to make a secondary bevel on the inside of the tool. To polish it, make a strop using a piece of dowel, or simply fold the leather in two or use its edge.*

9. How Often Do I Need to Sharpen My Tools?

This depends entirely on the density of the wood, whether or not you are using a mallet, how good the tool steel is at keeping an edge, and the design you are carving! Once again, there is no precise answer. It is best to assume that you will need to be frequently stropping your tool; so always have it on hand and freshly dressed.

As you gain experience, you will feel the tool getting blunt because it will need more energy to push through the wood, and you will probably see the results of a blunt tool also tearing the surface.

As the tool wears from normal usage, its cutting edge will become misshapen. It may become hollow in the middle, and it will probably become more and more convex on the bevel. A secondary bevel may also appear along the edge of the primary bevel. If these cannot be removed with the slip stone, reshaping on a grinding wheel will be necessary.

The sorts of wear typical of carving tools are shown in **A2-7**.

A2-7 *Eventually the tools will need some maintenance by reshaping them on a grinding wheel. A slip stone, used on a regular basis, will provide the majority of shape maintenance that is required on an ongoing basis.*

10. Should I Use Sharpening Jigs to Help Me?

A sharpening jig is a device that is designed to help hold the tool in the right position for grinding on a stone. There are many designs of these jigs available on the market, each with its own advantage.

The best advice about sharpening jigs is that, if you find one that you think will make you a better tool sharpener, then try it out. There are, however, at least two downsides to sharpening jigs that are worth considering:

First, they tend to restrict the movement of the tool to a certain pattern, removing any flexibility that might be needed to create a particular shape. If you are trying to make a compound convex curve, for example placing a slightly convex bevel shape on a gouge, then a jig may prevent you from doing this. Jigs mostly allow constant angle cutting only.

Second, by using jigs and tool rests, the feel for what you are doing is often largely lost, so you are relying totally on visual input for your sharpening activity. An experienced tool sharpener will also rely on hand feel as a guide through the shaping process; experience of this can only be gained by not using tool jigs and rests.

As a generalization, it is better to learn the process and gain the skill by freehand grinding and sharpening. If you achieve this, you will find that a sharpening jig or rest is most often a hindrance, both in time taken and end result.

11. What Is a Strop Used for?

The tool-sharpening process is made up of the three main areas of grinding on a wheel (for shaping and repairing), sharpening on a slip stone (for fine-tuning the bevel and creating a sharp edge), and honing on a strop (for polishing the face to a razor edge).

A scratched sharp edge will not be efficient for cutting through the wood. Leftover grinding marks (either from the wheel or the slip stone) will mean that the cutting edge has minute ruts in it, which if large enough will be visible on the wood surface as scratches. These need to be polished out.

A firm leather strop (not made from soft leather that will only squash under pressure and round off the

A2-8 Draw the tool down the length of the strop, rolling it on its curve as you go. Repeat several times, and you will soon see a polished surface on the tool.

sharp edge you have created) with a solid wood backboard and some very fine abrasive metal-polishing powder is all you need **(A2-8)**.

The difference in the carving performance from a tool that has been stropped to one that has not is considerable. Polish both sides of the cutting edge for best results.

12. How Do I Remove a Chip in a Tool Blade?

A chip is typically caused by tools knocking together in a tool pouch or drawer, by banging a tool against a hard metal surface, or by dropping the tool on the floor. Sometimes a chip might be severe enough to actually be at the end of a fracture in the blade. In this case, there is probably little that can be done to repair the damage.

To successfully remove a chip can often mean the removal of more than 1/16 inch (2mm) of metal from the end of the blade. The bevel also needs to be reinstated, so the regrinding can be significant. If it is at all possible, leave chip repair until it is absolutely necessary. For example, if you are roughing out a carving and it is of no consequence as to whether there are scratches all over the surface, then leave the repair until it becomes important. This way, the life of the tool is extended, sometimes significantly (because metal does not need to be ground away).

Note that most tools are only tempered for a short distance of an inch (25mm) or so of their length, so anything that saves steel is worth the effort.

13. What Happens If My Carving Tool Becomes Overheated?

The composition of the steel in the tool will determine the temperature and exposure time at which the strength of the steel in the tool becomes adversely affected by heat. The result of overheating is a loss of hardness or "temper" of the tool. The softer the steel becomes, the less effective it is at holding an edge, if it will do so at all.

The first thing you will notice is a blue-black discoloration on the surface of the steel **(A2-9)**. Rub the tool on a strop; if the discoloration is superficial and disappears, the tool is probably largely unaffected.

If the tool is overheated too much, the discoloration will be right through the steel and, of course, cannot be removed; the tool will be unable to sustain a sharp edge and will blunt or crumble very quickly under stress. If this occurs, regrind the tool by removing the affected area, effectively starting again. If the original damage was significant enough, the tool will not sustain any further grinding; it has become useless as a carving instrument.

14. I Keep on Sharpening; Why Doesn't My Chisel Get Any Better?

If you are frustrated by the apparent inability of your sharpening efforts to make the tool feel any better (more effective) in the wood, then the most likely reasons are:

You haven't "gone far enough" in your application of the process, and the tool isn't quite ground so that the two surfaces (the top surface and the bevel surface) actually meet to form a sharp edge.

Hold the tool so that you can see a bright light reflect off the sharp end of the blade. If you can see any shiny silver lines or spots, these are blunt areas, and you need to continue the sharpening process to remove them **(A2-10)**.

If there are no blunt spots, then chances are you have ground the tool in such a way that you have made the sharp end more convex than it should be for easy use of the tool. The greater the convexity of the bevel, the higher the angle of approach of the tool to the surface of the wood and the harder it is to push it across or through it.

A2-9 If the blue-black burning on the steel is severe enough, the steel in the tool will become very brittle and will crumble away under the stress of pressure on wood. The moment any discoloration is noticed during grinding, stop the activity immediately, and cool the tool down in some water. It is best to dip the tool in water every few seconds to ensure this does not occur.

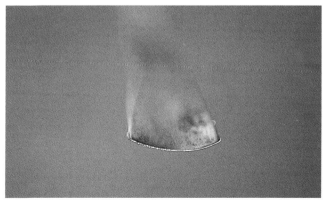

A2-10 The shiny edges you can see are blunt spots that need just a little more grinding away to make them sharp. A sharp edge will not reflect sufficient light for it to be seen by the naked eye. A blunt edge will show up as a shiny spot or line.

So, if you keep on sharpening too convex a curve or too acute an angle, all you will be doing is making the tool harder and harder to push through the wood, so that it feels like it is getting more and more blunt. It will feel quite sharp to the "finger touch," but it simply will not perform in wood. You can normally see this problem if you hold the bevel, in a good light, and examine the shape of it at the cutting edge. If it looks "round" then sharpen it flat or at least flatter, and it will improve its performance.

15. Should the Face of My Tools Be Flat or the Corners Round?

The shape of the face of the tool will depend on the function it is to perform. Most tools are manufactured flat across the face; this is satisfactory for a lot of work. A tool that is hollow, or concave, in the face is just about of no use at all for general work. A tool that is raked back at the shoulders, or has round shoulders, is the most flexible of all, particularly if you want to create rolling scrolls such as might appear in leaf and floral designs.

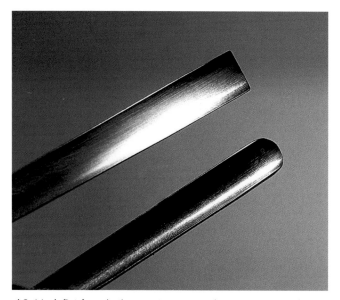

A2-11 A flat face is the most common; however, a rounded or raked-back shoulder offers the greatest flexibility and allows the tool to be easily used for rolling over during scroll work. A concave shape (hollow in the middle) is almost useless for just about every carving situation.

A raked-back tool has a shortcoming for undercutting (see Chapter 3) whereas a flat-faced tool is generally more effective. It is probably best to have a mixture of flat- and round-faced tools, for greatest flexibility. You will want flat faces for undercutting and for tools that you would use for stop cutting (see Chapter 3), and rounded shoulders for tools that are for shaping curves. This would apply to fluters and medium to deep gouges in particular and fine finishing tools where you want to avoid at all costs the corners of the tool digging in and damaging the cleanly finished surface.

Flat and curved-face chisels are shown in A2-11. If it is necessary for you to reshape the shoulders of any of your tools, be sure not to overheat them during the grinding process on a high-speed wheel.

16. How Do I Remove the Burr from the Cutting Edge?

A burr may be formed while using the grinding wheel or the slip stone. It is made up of steel that is rubbed or ground off the surface and rolled over the cutting edge. It will eventually break off as a fine sliver.

As soon as the bevel starts to form, it is the signal to stop grinding or sharpening, as any further activity will simply continue to unnecessarily remove steel. Rather than breaking it off or letting it fall off, it is best to remove it with your slip stone or strop. Carefully wipe the tool over the strop; if this doesn't remove the bevel, go back to the slip stone. Gently wipe the stone on the blade, being careful to hold the stone very flat so as not to accidentally create the beginnings of a secondary bevel on the tool. A secondary bevel will make the angle of approach at the cutting edge higher and make the tool less effective in the wood.

Once the burr is removed, check that there are no shiny spots or lines on the cutting edge. It may be that the burr was masking a flat spot.

17. How Do I Keep My Tools from Getting Rusty?

Rust can severely damage tools. If it pits the surfaces top or bottom down near the cutting edge, it may make it impossible to create a fine, clean cutting edge without chips that will cause scratching.

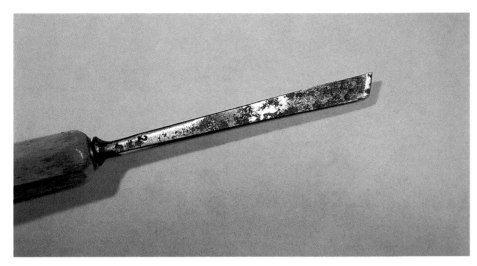

A2-12 Rust like this has pitted the steel and has made it impossible to polish to a sharp edge.

Sweat from your hands will cause rust formation, particularly as it is salty. A damp storage atmosphere is also an invitation for rust to pay a visit.

Ensure you wipe the tools before you finish a carving session, and store them in a dry environment such as a tool roll or tool box with a lid. Place some hygroscopic silica gel with the tools to attract any moisture that might otherwise begin rust formation.

A thin coat of Vaseline or oil will also prevent rust appearing. This should be wiped off before using the tools, as greasy substances will transfer from your hands to the wood and discolor it, making it look dirty. You could make your own rust-prevention coating by dissolving some gum turpentine, lard, and resin together in equal portions and smearing it on the tools. This will dry clear; it will not come off onto the wood and damage it (**A2-12**).

18. How Do I Sharpen My Knife?

Before you start to sharpen your knife, take a look at the bevel the manufacturer placed on it (**A2-13**). Some knives have a single bevel on one side only; others have a bevel on both sides. The bevels are often very short, making the tool hard to use.

The easiest knife to use for general carving work is one with a bevel on both sides. Make the bevel wide so that the blade has a long, thin cross section, and it will take off the finest shavings in most woods. This kind of blade will also be easily damaged, so it is important to protect it during storage and not to have too high an expectation of its performance in harder wood. Try a shorter bevel in harder timbers, as this will not be so inclined to chip, serrate, or even bend or break.

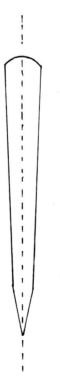

A2-13 Similarly to the carving chisel, the knife will perform more easily if the bevel is long and thin. It will also damage more easily. For harder wood, try a double-bevel blade (i.e., one with a bevel on both sides).

19. How Do I Get My Skew to Work Properly?

If your skew is sharp, but doesn't seem to want to work properly, chances are its bevels are the wrong shape and/or the angle at which it is skewed is too large. This tool is awkward to use until you get used to it. If the bevels are too round, it will be very difficult to get it to do what you want. A bevel that is too convex will slide off the surface of the wood and be difficult to get to cut.

A bevel that is flat will be a lot easier to use, and one that is slightly concave or hollow ground will in many circumstances be easiest to use. It is a matter of experimentation and choice of the bevel shape that best suits your style for holding the tool. To hollow-grind the tool, sharpen it on the circumference edge of the wheel (the edge that faces you), unlike all the other carving tools that you will sharpen on the flat face of the wheel that faces to your right or left.

Start with a flat bevel, since this is the easiest to create and maintain, and, chances are, it will work perfectly for you (A2-14). A good average skew angle is about 30 degrees. This will of course once again depend on the individual, so start with about 45 degrees and work backwards from there, regrinding the bevels each time you alter the angle. It would be most practical to establish your most comfortable bevel first, and then establish the best angle of skew.

20. How Do I Sharpen My V Tool?

The V tool is really a gouge with high, flat sides. If you examine the inside of the tool where the apex is, you will notice that it is ever so slightly round; it does not come to a point at all. It is necessary to shape the outside of the tool to match the shape of the inside of the tool so a sharp edge is formed at the apex. Otherwise a blunt spot will remain, and the tool will tear the surface of the wood.

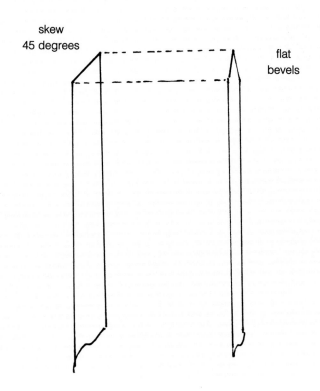

skew
45 degrees

flat
bevels

A2-14 Trial and error is about the only way to find the optimum combination of skew and bevel angles. Start with long flat bevels and a skew of about 45 degrees. Try altering the skew angle toward 30 degrees if 45 degrees is too difficult to use. If the tool slides off the wood, the bevels are most likely too convex.

Sharpen the tool as though it were a gouge, by rolling the apex over the slip stone just as you would a gouge (**A2-15**). Wipe any burr from the inside of the tool with the flat edge of the stone.

It is very important to avoid rubbing the slip stone into the inside of the apex and, literally, digging a hole in it. If this happens, it will most likely be necessary to regrind the tool; however, try it first in case it does work without tearing the wood, otherwise you will be wasting metal.

If the outside bevels of the tool are too vigorously ground on a wheel or a slip stone, it is possible to wear them away and, in so doing, form a shape like the prow of a boat at the cutting edge. This also may require regrinding. Care in the grinding process is best to prevent these mishaps occurring.

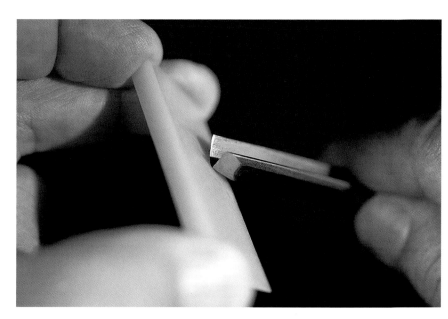

A2-15 To prevent a blunt spot at the apex, roll the tool over the slip stone as you would a gouge. Be careful when removing any burr from the inside not to dig a hole in the apex, and ensure care in grinding the bevels so as not to form a point like the prow of a boat. This will wear or break off and cause tearing of the wood surface.

APPENDIX 3
Essential Tools for the Projects & How to Hold Them

As we have previously mentioned there are hundreds of different shapes of carving tool and thousands of other tools you can choose from to make the various activities you do that much easier.

All of this can be very confusing to begin with; at the end of the day you will come to realize that you don't really need that many at all to have a lot of productive and creative fun with carving wood.

Throughout this book we have kept the tool requirements to a minimum; in this Appendix we collectively show the specific woodcarving tools that are essential.

CHISELS & KNIVES

You will need chisels like the ones in **A3-1** to complete Chapters 1, 2, 3, 4, 6, 7, and 9. To complete Chapter 10, you will need to add the tools in **A3-2**. To complete Chapter 13, you will need to add the two tools shown in **A3-3**.

For the chip carving in Chapter 8, you can use standard chisels and a skew, but you will find the going much easier if you add a hook-nosed cutting knife and a stab knife like those shown in **A3-4**.

A3-1 Chisels like these are needed for Chapters 1, 2, 3, 4, 6, 7, and 9. Left to right they are a ⅞-inch almost flat gouge, a ⅞-inch skew, a ½-inch almost flat gouge, a ⅛-inch fluter, a ¼-inch V tool, and a whittling knife.

A3-2 Additional tools needed for Chapter 10. On the left is a ½-inch long bent, almost flat gouge; on the right is a ¼-inch almost flat gouge.

A3-3 *Two extra tools for Chapter 13. On the left is a 2-inch almost flat gouge and on the right is a ⅝-inch reasonably round gouge.*

Storing Your Tools

There are several different storage systems available for carving tools. A tool roll is a popular choice; however, the safest and most convenient storage is a tray like the one shown in **A3-5**.

A3-4 *The hook-nosed cutting knife at the top and the stab knife below are especially suited for chip carving, such as that in Chapter 8.*

A3-5 *A tray is the safest, most convenient storage system of the many available for carving tools.*

A3-6 *A woodcarver's mallet is necessary for the control of your tools. The one on the left is useful for people who have arthritis and should not try to hold a handle. The other mallets are made from a hard wood that eventually pulverizes.*

MALLETS & HOW TO USE THEM

For control of your tools, you will need to purchase a woodcarver's mallet, like one of those in **A3-6**. Choose one that weighs about 16 ounces (450 grams).

Strike your mallet on the chisel handle with a positive stroke that is at right angles to the shaft of the chisel (**A3-7**). Avoid a striking posture that delivers the mallet to the handle in a glancing blow, as shown in **A3-8**. It will take half an hour or so to get used to holding and using your mallet, so be patient.

A3-9 *Do this. This is a correct holding position for someone who is right-handed; the chisel is being held in the left hand with the mallet in the right. The wrist of the left hand rests on the wood being carved for maximum control.*

A3-7 *Do this. The correct way to strike your mallet on the chisel handle: using a positive stroke that is at right angles to the shaft of the chisel.*

A3-8 *NOT this. This is an incorrect striking posture; it delivers the mallet to the handle in a glancing blow.*

A3-10 *NOT this. This is an incorrect holding position; the chisel held high up on the handle reduces your tool control and the gouge tends to wobble around.*

The person in **A3-9** is right-handed, so the chisel is being held in the left hand with the mallet in the right. The wrist of the left hand rests on the wood being carved for maximum control. If you hold the chisel high up on the handle as shown **A3-10**, your tool control will be reduced and the gouge will tend to wobble around. Pay attention to the way you are holding your tools and you will naturally develop proper habits.

Controling the Tool When Not Using a Mallet

Even when you are not using a mallet, keep in mind that the greatest tool control is achieved by resting your hand on the carving wood (**A3-11**). Place both your hands comfortably around the tool as you rest your wrist or hand on the carving or you run the risk of not being able to control your tool satisfactorily (**A3-12**).

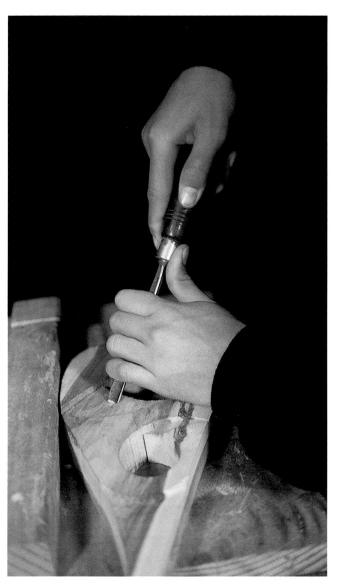

A3-11 Do this. Place both your hands comfortably around the tool when not using a mallet, and rest your hand on the carving wood to achieve the greatest tool control.

A3-12 NOT this. You may not be able to control your tool satisfactorily if you do not rest your wrist or hand on the carving.

SHARPENING

For sharpening you will need a slip stone (**A3-13**), as described in Appendix 2. Make sure you hold it comfortably, and so you can see what you are doing. Also as described in Appendix 2, you will need a leather strop for polishing (**A3-14**). Always keep safety in mind: Be careful not to cut the hand that is holding the strop, and do not hold the tool at too high an angle, otherwise you will blunt the edge.

OTHER ESSENTIAL TOOLS

For cutting profiles, you will need to purchase a coping saw (**A3-15**), unless you have access to a scroll saw or a band saw.

Holding Devices

You will need at least two G clamps (**A3-16**) for holding boards attached to the base of your work onto your bench or tabletop. Purchase clamps that have an open-

A3-13 A slip stone is needed for sharpening, as described in Appendix 2.

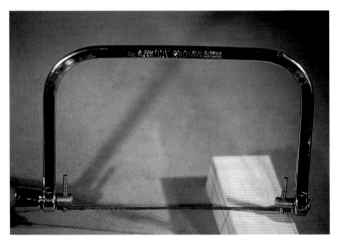

A3-15 A coping saw is needed for cutting profiles unless you have access to a scroll saw or a band saw.

A3-14 A leather strop is needed for polishing and should be used with care. Maintain the proper low angle to ensure the edge is not dulled, and watch out for the hand holding the strop to avoid cuts.

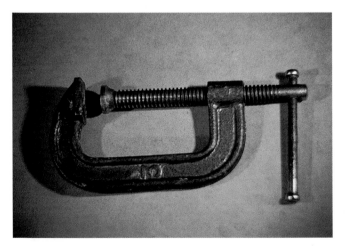

A3-16 G clamps are essential for holding boards onto your bench or tabletop. One of the most useful methods for holding carvings is to attach a board to the base of the carving and then use G clamps to hold the assembly firm.

A3-17 A homemade bench hook is useful for holding carving as well as for holding wood while you cut it with a tenon or similar saw.

ing of about 4 inches. Always place a thin scrap of wood between the jaw and the carving and be careful that the pressure from clamping will not split the wood.

You will need a bench hook (**A3-17**), a simple homemade device for holding your carving while you work on it. It is no more than a flat base about ¾ inch thick, with a cleat glued and screwed on each edge; one on the top for resting the carving on and the other on the bottom for pushing up against the edge of your bench or table.

Sanding Accessories
If you find sanding with paper difficult, for example if you suffer from arthritis, there are many products like the sanding drums in **A3-18** that may help you. These can be used with a power source, such as a flexile shaft attached to an electric drill.

A3-18 Sanding drums and many other products may be useful if you find sanding with paper difficult. A rotary tool or an electric drill with a flexible shaft make these accessories convenient to use.

APPENDIX 4
Common & Botanical Names of Wood

[Cultivated in the United States & Canada]

APPLE (Fruit)	*Malus* spp.
ASH (Silver)	*Flindersia bourjotiana*
BALSA	*Ochroma pyramidale*
BASSWOOD (Lime)	*Tilia* spp.
BEECH	
(American)	*Fagus sylvatica*
(Southern)	*Nothofagus cunninghamii*
(White)	*Gmelina leichardtii*
CEDAR	
(Eastern red)	*Juniperus virginiana*
(of Lebanon)	*Cedrus libani*
(True)	*Cedrela [Toona]* spp.
(Western red)	*Thuja plicata*
CHERRY	*Prunus avium*
COCOBOLO	*Dalbergia retusa*
DOUGLAS FIR	*Pseudotsuga menziesii*
ELM	*Ulmus* spp.
JELUTONG	*Dyera costulata*
KAURI	
(Pine)	*Agathis australis*
(Tropical)	*Agathis dammara*
LAUREL (Camphor)	*Cinnamomum camphora*
LINDEN (Lime)	*Tilia* spp.
MAHOGANY	
(African)	*Khaya* spp.
(Honduran)	*Swietenia macrophylla*

MYRTLE	*Myrtus communis*
NEEDLEWOOD	*Grevillia* spp.
OAK	
(American red)	*Quercus rubra*
(American white)	*Quercus alba*
OLIVE	*Olea europaea*
OSAGE ORANGE	*Maclura pomifera*
PADAUK	*Pterocarpus indicus*
PEAR	*Pyrus communis*
PINE	
(Baltic)	*Picea abies*
(Eastern white)	*Pinus strobus*
(Huon)	*Dacrydium franklinii*
(Oregon sugar)	*Pseudosuga menziesii*
(Quebec, yellow)	*Pinus strobus*
(Radiata)	*Pinus radiata*
POPLAR	*Populus alba*
PURPLEHEART	*Peltogyne* spp.
ROSEWOOD	*Dalbergia* spp.
SASSAFRAS	*Sassafras albidum*
TEAK	*Tectona grandis*
WALNUT (Black)	*Juglans nigra*
WATTLE (Gidgee)	*Acacia cambegei*
WILLOW (Black)	*Salix nigra*
YEW (English)	*Taxus baccata*
ZEBRAWOOD	*Microberlinia brazzavillensis*

APPENDIX 5
Metric Equivalents

[to the nearest 1mm, 0.1cm, 0.001m]

inches	mm	cm		inches	mm	cm
⅛	3	0.3		12	305	30.5
¼	6	0.6		13	330	33.0
⅜	10	1.0		14	356	35.6
½	13	1.3		15	381	38.1
⅝	16	1.6		16	406	40.6
¾	19	1.9		17	432	43.2
⅞	22	2.2		18	457	45.7
1	25	2.5		19	483	48.3
1¼	32	3.2		20	508	50.8
1½	38	3.8		21	533	53.3
1¾	44	4.4		22	559	55.9
2	51	5.1		23	584	58.4
2½	64	6.4		24	610	61.0
3	76	7.6		25	635	63.5
3½	89	8.9		26	660	66.0
4	102	10.2				
4½	114	11.4		inches	feet	m
5	127	12.7				
6	152	15.2		12	1	0.305
7	178	17.8		24	2	0.610
8	203	20.3		36	3	0.914
9	229	22.9		48	4	1.219
10	254	25.4		60	5	1.524
11	279	27.9				

Conversion Factors

mm	=	millimeter		m	=	meter
cm	=	centimeter		m^2	=	square meter
1 mm	=	0.039 inch		1 inch	=	25.4 mm
1 m	=	3.28 feet		1 foot	=	304.8 mm
1 m^2	=	10.8 square feet		1 sq ft	=	0.09 m^2

INDEX